The European Community and American Trade

A STUDY IN ATLANTIC ECONOMICS AND POLICY

RANDALL HINSHAW

The European Community and American Trade

A STUDY IN ATLANTIC ECONOMICS AND POLICY

Published for the
Council on Foreign Relations
by FREDERICK A. PRAEGER, *Publishers*
New York • *Washington* • *London*

FREDERICK A. PRAEGER, Publishers
111 Fourth Avenue, New York 3, N.Y., U.S.A.
77-79 Charlotte Street, London W.1, England

THE EUROPEAN COMMUNITY AND AMERICAN TRADE: A STUDY IN ATLANTIC
ECONOMICS AND POLICY

Published in the United States of America in 1964
by Frederick A. Praeger, Inc., Publishers

FIRST EDITION

Library of Congress catalog card number: 64-25588
Printed in the United States of America
by Capital City Press, Inc., Montpelier, Vermont

For a list of Council publications see pages 186, and 187.

Preface

This is a book about the Common Market and related developments in Western Europe from the standpoint of the United
States. It is an economic study in the sense that it attempts to
shed light on the impact of European integration on American
and, more broadly, on Atlantic economic strength. At the same
time, it is a wider study in the sense that it seeks to derive, from
non-economic as well as from economic considerations, the implications of European integration for American trade policy, not
only in relation to Western Europe, but in relation to the non-
Communist world as a whole—including the broad group of low-
income countries that account for most of its population.

Writing about the living is a proverbially perilous undertaking;
writing about emerging institutions, I have painfully learned, is
at least as hazardous. It would be an understatement to say that
the rapidly changing factual background has been a source of
continual concern and, at times, dismay. Certain issues that
seemed important when this study was begun in 1959 have faded
into oblivion, and the same fate doubtless awaits some of the
problems on which attention is centered today. I have tried to
minimize these difficulties by concentrating on longer range

questions—questions which, if present indications are not too deceiving, should be of major significance for the next decade or two.

While I hope it will interest them, the book is aimed at a much wider audience than my fellow economists. Accordingly, I have taken pains to avoid needless academic and technical jargon, including the rapidly developing jargon originating in Brussels and elsewhere on specialized aspects of European integration. In tackling such a broad subject, it has been necessary to discuss many matters, often of exasperating complexity, on which I am not a specialist, and I can only hope that a kind fate has saved me from egregious errors of fact or judgment.

My debts to others, by no means all of which are here recorded, can only be described as immense. I would first like to acknowledge my profound appreciation to the Council on Foreign Relations for making possible a project in which I could unite my interest in Western European and Atlantic affairs with my interest in commercial policy. From the beginning, I have at all times been keenly aware of the Council's unwavering support and encouragement, particularly during the many months when I seemed to be in a losing race with the march of events.

Under its usual procedure, the Council appointed a Study Group of great distinction, reflecting a broad spectrum of views and interests. Members of the group included Henry G. Aubrey, George W. Ball, Robert W. Barnett, Roy M. Blough, William Butler, William Diebold, Jr., Isaiah Frank, David M. Freudenthal, Lincoln Gordon, Andrew M. Kamarck, Walter J. Levy, Harold F. Linder, David W. MacEachron, William J. Mazzocco, John D. Montgomery, Ben T. Moore, Gardner Patterson, the late Michael Ross, Nathaniel Samuels, Walter J. Sedwitz, Whitney H. Shepardson, Leroy D. Stinebower, Edward Townsend, Howard P. Whidden, and John H. Williams. The group was most fortunate in having as chairman Alfred C. Neal, who, with great skill, brought to light many a question that might otherwise have escaped attention. The monthly meetings in 1959-60 were of immense value in stimulating my thinking in new directions, and there have since been many times when I have felt the need for further exchange of views with this remarkably astute group.

As part of the project, the Council made possible a trip to Europe in the spring of 1960, during which I had the opportunity to talk with government officials, political observers, and some of the principal architects of European integration. In Paris, I spent a memorable hour with Jean Monnet, and received much useful counsel from his able and gracious assistant, François Duchêne. I also profited greatly from talks with Raymond Aron, with Olivier Wormser of the French Foreign Office, and with Paul Winkler and Charles Ronsac of Opera Mundi, the French business research organization. Raymond Bertrand and other members of the OEEC (now OECD) Secretariat provided helpful background on regional developments in Western Europe. As elsewhere, I was greatly assisted by American officials, among whom I would especially like to name Jacques J. Reinstein, Clarence E. Hunter, and my esteemed friend and former Paris colleague, Ethel Dietrich, long the distinguished United States Representative on the OEEC Steering Board for Trade.

In Brussels, I first called on W. Walton Butterworth, Jr., then United States Ambassador to the European Economic Community, who was most helpful in explaining and interpreting the political aspects of European integration. He and his able staff—among whom I must name Dean Hinton, Bernard Norwood, and Oscar Zaglits—were of great assistance in providing information and in enabling me to make the best use of my time in the Common Market capital. At the EEC headquarters, I had a long and instructive conversation with President Walter Hallstein, who carefully explained Community policies toward the United States and other non-member countries. On the same subject, I also learned much from Jean François Deniau and others of the EEC staff. I would like to acknowledge my special debt to Richard Mayne for helpful counsel and gracious hospitality. Finally, my stay in Brussels was greatly enriched by a conversation with Max Kohnstamm, who has served the Common Market countries in various high positions. From my hour with this brilliant and dedicated official, I was able to see the problems and aspirations of the Community in a new light.

Contact with such persuasive Common Market advocates would indeed have threatened my objectivity if I had not made a serious effort to obtain the views of officials and observers in non-EEC countries. In Geneva, I received wise counsel on commercial policy questions concerning the Community from Eric Wyndham White, Executive Secretary of the General Agreement on Tariffs and Trade. Frederick Strauss and members of his knowledgeable staff at the Economic Commission for Europe discussed with me the Common Market and related developments from a United Nations point of view. From Acting Secretary-General Sten Lindh of the European Free Trade Association, I learned the EFTA position on various important issues.

In London, I continued my discussion of EFTA matters, and explored British attitudes toward the Common Market. Sir Richard Powell, Permanent Secretary of the Board of Trade, provided much useful background on the British position with respect to European integration. From Richard Bailey and his expert staff of the British research organization, PEP (Political and Economic Planning), I received a great deal of valuable economic analysis of British and EFTA problems. I benefited greatly from a conversation with Miriam Camps on EEC-EFTA relations and from a discussion on Western European agricultural policies with E. M. H. Lloyd, former Under Secretary of the British Ministry of Food. At the American Embassy, I received much kind assistance and counsel from Wilson T. M. Beale, Jr., and his staff, and from my good friend and former Federal Reserve colleague, Robert W. Bean, United States Treasury Representative.

My obligations in the United States are also numerous. On several trips to Washington, I profited greatly from discussions with many government and international officials, among whom I should name Stanley M. Cleveland, Arthur A. Hartman, John Leddy, and Leonard Weiss of the Department of State; Brian Rose of the International Monetary Fund; and my wise friends, Ralph C. Wood of the Federal Reserve Board, and Evan Hannay, trade adviser at the Treasury Department. With characteristic thoughtfulness, Leonard Tennyson, who ably represents the Community in Washington, has been a continuous source of information and encouragement. While they were in the United States, I obtained much helpful counsel on British and Commonwealth matters from Sir John Crawford, former Australian Minister of Trade, and from Shaun Stewart, Principal, United Kingdom Board of Trade.

Of the Council staff, I am indebted to many for helpfulness of various kinds. During my year in New York, George S. Franklin, Jr., and Philip E. Mosely offered wise counsel and, in their friendly way, did much to make the year a memorably pleasant experience. Under Ruth Savord and later under Donald Wasson, the Council library was of immense assistance in providing information on a long array of subjects. Helena Stalson, Council economist, gave excellent advice on questions of statistical presentation and other matters, and Robert Valkenier made many helpful editorial suggestions.

John H. Williams and Ben T. Moore read the manuscript of the book for the Council, and offered most helpful advice and encouragement. It must be emphasized, however, that none of the individuals here mentioned is in any way responsible for the content or conclusions of the book; for better or worse, the responsibility is exclusively mine.

My debt to my wife is immeasurable, and I will not attempt to list the many ways in which she has lightened my burden during the years that I have been involved in this project.

I cannot finish this preface without a word of special tribute to William Diebold, Jr., gentleman and scholar. His invariably fruitful suggestions, his rare good judgment, his patience with delay, and his unfailing interest and encouragement have made my task immensely easier.

RANDALL HINSHAW

July 1, 1964

Contents

List of Tables

xv

The European Community and American Trade

A STUDY IN ATLANTIC ECONOMICS AND POLICY

1

Grand Design or Grand Illusion?

We shall have peace when we have a United States of Europe.

CARLO CATTANEO, 1848

Faire l'Europe, c'est faire la paix.

JEAN MONNET, 1953

Now what are the realities of Europe? What are the pillars on which it can be built? Its constituent states are certainly very different from one another: each has its own spirit, its own history, its own language, its own misfortunes, glories, and ambitions; but these states are the only entities that have the right to make decrees and the authority to act. To imagine that we can create effective means of action, supported by the peoples, above and beyond the member states is nothing but an illusion.

CHARLES DE GAULLE, 1960

Prior to the abrupt turn of events initiated by President de Gaulle in early 1963, no development in recent years had inspired more hope—for Americans as well as for Europeans—than the emergence of the European Economic Community, less formally known as the Common Market. In a world which had become unaccustomed to good news, this remarkable achievement had already done much to restore faith in the possibilities of free institutions not merely as an attractive, but as an effective, alternative to communism. It was particularly heartening, moreover, that the Common Market was a Western European development; for, only a few years earlier, Western Europe had been regarded

3

by many Americans as perpetually cast in the role of an honored but impecunious relative, whose glories were mainly in the past and whose continued existence would probably require—whatever the euphemisms employed to avoid such terms—either a permanent subsidy from the United States or an environment permanently sheltered from the full blast of American competition.

Initiated as an economic arrangement, the Community was regarded by its architects—among whom the foremost was the great Frenchman, Jean Monnet—as the nucleus of a United States of Europe which, like the United States of America, would enjoy internal free trade over a large area and, in time, political union. Because it was expected to make a spectacular contribution to the economic strength and political unity of Western Europe, and therefore to Atlantic ability to defend the non-Communist world, the Common Market was strongly supported by the American government under both Republican and Democratic administrations. Founded by six continental nations with a combined population slightly less than that of the United States, the Community was expected to expand greatly in area and population if, as seemed probable, the United Kingdom and other excluded Western European countries were shortly to become members. For Americans, the prospective membership of Britain gave confidence that the Community would not become a tightly knit, "inward-looking," protectionist economic bloc, but would join the United States in an "Atlantic Partnership" which, by the appeal of its globally oriented policies, would assure a bright future for the free world.

While "shattered" would be too strong a word, these high hopes were rudely shaken by President de Gaulle's sudden termination of the negotiations on Britain's application for Common Market membership. For the time being, a point of view has triumphed which regards the future of the Community in very

4

different terms from those which have just been outlined. A careful reading of the remarks made by the French President at his now famous press conference of January 14, 1963, makes it clear that he viewed with mistrust and disfavor precisely those "outward-looking" tendencies within the Community which had so strongly appealed to Americans. To De Gaulle, Britain was unwelcome as a Common Market member because its interests were global rather than mainly European, and because these interests were closely linked with those of the United States. The inclusion of Britain and other currently excluded Western European countries would confront the Community, in De Gaulle's words, "with the problems of its economic relations with all sorts of other nations and, first of all, with the United States." This pattern of evolution, he predicted, would lead to "a colossal Atlantic community, dependent upon a control by the United States, and which would have absorbed the community of Europe." While such an outcome, he said, could "be perfectly justified in the eyes of some," it was "not at all what France wanted to do and is doing."

In his remarks on economic issues the French President made no effort to hide his conception of the Common Market as a protectionist economic bloc. After pointing out that Britain is largely dependent for its supply of food on imports "bought cheaply in the two Americas and in the dominions," he asked, rhetorically, how Britain could be brought into the "system of the Six," which "consists of treating agricultural products of the whole Community as a whole, of vigorously fixing their prices, . . . of organizing their consumption among all members and obliging each to pay into the Community" the saving that "they would achieve by bringing in foodstuffs from the outside instead of getting what the Common Market offers." A balder statement of the protectionist basis of Common Market agricultural policies could hardly be devised by the Community's harshest critics.

Without passing judgment at this point on these forcefully

expressed conclusions of De Gaulle, it is plain that they reflect a very different conception of the future role of the Community from that held, until 1963, by the Eisenhower and Kennedy administrations. Moreover, it is plain that, for the time being, De Gaulle's views have prevailed. This does not mean, of course, that they will continue to prevail, but it does mean that certain optimistic propositions which were almost taken for granted until 1963 must now be stated, not as foregone conclusions, but as unanswered questions.

That the White House view of the proper role of the Community could be radically different from that held in the Elysée Palace is not in itself especially surprising since the Common Market is the result of a complex set of forces, some of which have pushed in opposite directions. In the early postwar years the movement toward European integration, of which the Common Market is a spectacular manifestation, was a pragmatic reaction to the crushing problems of European reconstruction—problems which revealed to the most obtuse the utter inadequacy of uncoordinated national action. In addition, the dollar shortage which prevailed during these years provided a justification for a strictly regional (i.e., intra-European) attack on trade barriers, unaccompanied for the time being by any effort to remove barriers against the outside world. In some degree the integrating influences during this period were "inward-looking," because there was an important body of opinion on both sides of the Atlantic which expected the dollar shortage to continue indefinitely. This point of view remained influential until the late 1950s, and many who shared it held that a high level of trade protection against the outside world, and particularly against the United States, should be a permanent feature of Western European integration.

By 1950 the disturbing question of the future role of Germany provided a strong new impetus to European integration. The Schuman Plan, which was proposed in that year by France, was an effort to put an end to the long, tragic history of Franco-German strife by placing the coal and steel resources of the two countries, and other participants, under supranational management. Thus was born the "Little Europe" of the Six. The Schuman Plan was proposed just a few weeks before the outbreak of the Korean conflict, which added yet another powerful motive for European integration: the overriding need for increasing the economic strength and political unity of Western Europe in order to achieve a more effective defense of the non-Communist world. Indeed, without the long years of intensified cold war which followed the hot war in Korea, it is doubtful that the political solidarity required to establish the European Economic Community would have emerged.

With European reconstruction brilliantly achieved, with the dollar shortage a rapidly receding memory, with Franco-German partnership a reality, and with the cold war perhaps assuming a less somber quality, the time would appear to be ripe for a new examination of the Common Market in terms of American interests. Such an examination is attempted in the present volume in an effort to determine the major implications for American trade policy. Admittedly, this is a formidable undertaking, for American interests in relation to the Community are to some extent in apparent conflict, and any statement of such interests that gets down to particulars is bound to be controversial. But the task is important; indeed, there are few matters on which the United States will have a greater need for skillful and creative statesmanship.

At this stage it will be useful to attempt a statement—for the time being a very brief, general, and preliminary statement—of American interests as they relate to the European Economic Community. Whatever its shortcomings may be, this procedure has the advantage of revealing from the outset the main questions with which this volume will be concerned.

The United States, the Common Market, and the Free World

The first proposition, which is perhaps less a judgment than a simple statement of fact, is that the United States, because of its pre-eminent wealth and power, has inherited the mantle of leadership of the free world—a role which affects its interest in the Common Market in several distinct ways. The term "free world" is here used without apology as a convenient expression to include all those countries which are free from Communist domination. Thus defined, the free world accounts for about two-thirds of the world's population and, to say the least, is an exceedingly heterogeneous collection of countries revealing, in particular, an enormous disparity in economic well-being. For present purposes the non-Communist world may be divided into two groups: a group of relatively rich countries including the United States, most of Western Europe, Canada, Australia, New Zealand, and— as a borderline case— Japan; and a group of poor—in many cases, desperately poor—countries embracing most of Africa, most of Latin America, and most of non-Communist Asia. In population, the poor countries far outnumber the rich, accounting in turn for about two-thirds of the inhabitants of the free world. In its policies toward the Common Market, and particularly in determining the character of any association or "partnership" with the Community, the United States must be sensitive to the aspirations of the low-income countries not only because of the number of human beings involved, but also because these countries, with their often appalling human misery, are particularly vulnerable to the appeal of communism.

Leadership of the free world is a position of immense responsibility but also of immense opportunity, and it requires little wisdom to perceive that much depends on how the role is played. The stakes, indeed, are incalculably high. As a member and as leader of the free world, the United States is engaged in a contest

8

with the Communist world which may last for generations and which, hopefully, will ultimately be resolved, not in a Pyrrhic victory at some nuclear Armageddon, but in the eventual supremacy of free institutions because of their greater appeal and their superior capacity to meet human needs. But however long this contest may be, and whatever its future shape, the present task confronting the leadership of the free world is to achieve and maintain an increasingly attractive *modus vivendi*, within which the aspirations of the poor countries as well as the rich are given the greatest possible scope for realization.

European Integration and Atlantic Strength

To maintain such a *modus vivendi*, the free world must first of all be strong. Militarily, it must be strong enough to defend itself; in contemporary terms this means that it must be strong enough to deter nuclear attack. Over the long run defensive strength will depend on economic strength, particularly on the economic strength of those nations—notably the United States and its Atlantic partners—which must bear the actual military burdens. It should be emphasized that economic strength, in this context, must be conceived in dynamic terms. Thus, if production within the Communist world is expanding at an average annual rate of x per cent, production within those countries defending the free world must expand at a comparable rate if their relative economic strength is not to deteriorate. This does not necessarily mean that the cold war must be accepted as a permanent feature of the international scene, or that mankind must perpetually live with the recent degree of international tension. But it does mean that any lasting political equilibrium between the Communist and the non-Communist worlds will surely require an economic equilibrium in which the free world continues to remain economically strong in relation to the Communist bloc.

In this connection the emergence of the Common Market clear-

9

ly has major implications. On the one hand, it has been contended that the Common Market will make a spectacular contribution to the economic strength of Western Europe. On the other hand, it is feared on this side of the Atlantic that the Common Market may have an unfavorable effect on the economic strength of the United States. The first proposition, which clearly can no longer be stated as a foregone conclusion but must be phrased as a question, will be examined at length in Chapter 4. The second subject, which also needs to be re-examined in the light of recent developments, is elaborated in Chapter 8.

Essential to an adequate analysis of the impact of the Common Market on Atlantic economic strength is a knowledge of the existing and prospective pattern of Atlantic tariffs. This factual background is provided in Chapter 5.

The Common Market and Atlantic Unity

In achieving a brighter future for the free world, military and economic strength, while essential, are not enough. There must also be a high degree of solidarity, particularly among those countries which share the major responsibility for Western defense.

Here the Community has thus far had a decidedly ambivalent history. Like the Schuman Plan, it has played a noble role in putting an end to old enmities and in promoting that cooperation between France and Germany that is now so easily taken for granted. Nevertheless, the Community, apart from being the source of bitter internal disputes which have threatened to paralyze its development, has at least temporarily led to an increase in economic and political friction between those Western European countries that are members of the arrangement and those that are not. The present division of Western Europe into two large rival regional groupings (the European Economic Community of the Six and the European Free Trade Association of the Seven) is a far from satisfactory development on the road toward a united Europe; and while it is easy to exaggerate the economic dislocations that have thus far taken place as a result of the attendant tariff changes, it is likewise easy to underestimate the political dangers—in particular, the threat to effective Atlantic cooperation.

For a time this problem appeared to be well on the way to a solution, in view of the expected enlargement of the Community to include Britain and other Western European countries. The road, however, has for the time being been blocked by President de Gaulle, and the complex problem of the relationship of Britain to the Community remains unsolved. This problem, which presents the foremost threat to Western European unity, will be reconsidered in Chapter 6.

To some, the ultimate solution to the problem of Atlantic solidarity is an Atlantic Economic Community, in which the Common Market would eventually be expanded to include the presently excluded countries of Western Europe, the United States, and Canada. We shall examine this approach, in which there are a number of possible variations, in Chapter 9. For the time being, of course, the discussion of such a possibility is a highly academic exercise, if only because of President de Gaulle's vehement opposition to it. Yet as a prescription for American policy, membership in an Atlantic Community has an undeniable appeal as a straightforward, comprehensive approach to the objective of Atlantic solidarity. At the same time there is the danger that such an organization—if it were to assume the form, for example, of a customs union—would be regarded by the poorer countries of the free world as a rich man's club. Indeed, it is hard to see how they could regard it otherwise if the United States were to move toward free trade with Western Europe and Canada while retaining protection against nations which, in almost every case, would be in the low-income category.

It is here that American policy needs to be formulated with particular care, for the free world must not only be strong; it must also offer a more attractive future, particularly to its poorer members, than is offered by the Communist world. Defections from the free world by the rich countries, after all, are not a major threat. But defections by the poor countries cannot be ruled out; and for these countries in the throes of economic growth the Common Market, whether in its present or in an expanded form, cannot be regarded as an unmixed blessing. On the contrary, it poses certain serious problems.

European Integration and the Poor Nations

The problem which has thus far received the most attention in this connection concerns the trade discrimination which will be suffered by those among the less developed countries that are not associated with the Community. Members of the Community have agreed to extend free trade not only to one another, but also to the non-European countries with which they have "special relations"—that is to say, to their present and former dependencies in the tropics and elsewhere, most of which have recently become independent countries. Under this arrangement the products of former French colonies in tropical Africa, for example, will have free access to the markets not only of France, but also of the other members of the Community. This state of affairs will be fine, needless to say, for the countries that have a tie with the Common Market, but will make life more difficult for the low-income countries that have no such tie. For the United States the matter is of special concern, since the tropical countries of Latin America are among those that will suffer most from the new tariff preferences.

This arrangement between the Community and its "associated

overseas countries and territories," however reasonable it may have seemed to its creators when the Rome Treaty was drafted, is surely an anachronism now. To minimize the trade discrimination that it would involve, President Kennedy proposed that the United States and the Community jointly agree to extend free trade in those tropical products where no important domestic producing interest is involved. This proposal, which has been incorporated in the Trade Expansion Act of 1962, is excellent as far as it goes and, if accepted by the Community, would do much to remove the specific problem here described.

But the commercial problems confronting the low-income countries are of a broader character than trade discrimination in tropical products. Like the rich nations, the poor countries want to achieve a higher rate of economic growth—not, primarily, to maintain or to increase their relative power status but to alleviate their frightening human misery. Economic growth, however, will entail a continuous growth of imports and, if these are to be paid for on a self-supporting basis, the poor countries will need steadily expanding markets for their exports.

It would be a serious over-simplification of the problem to assume that this is merely a matter of finding increased markets for tropical products, or even for primary products as a whole. In the case of tropical food products, as Barbara Ward has observed, there is a limit, even under free trade, to the expansibility of the stomachs of the rich. In any event, the low-income countries regard themselves as excessively dependent on exports of primary products, which in many cases are subject to enormous price variations, and they are inclined to view the traditional pattern of trade—that is, the exchange of their primary products for the manufactured goods of the high-income countries—as a relic of colonialism. The industrial revolution is overtaking many of the poor nations, some of which are already highly competitive in certain types of manufactured goods.

13

These observations, of course, bring us squarely face to face with the problem of "low-wage goods," a problem which the developed countries usually think of only from their own point of view. Indeed, their standard approach is to devise ways and means to minimize purchases of manufactured goods from the low-income countries—an approach which, in the case of textiles, has achieved a high degree of ingenuity. Even when disposed to move toward freer trade, the developed countries typically regard low-wage manufactures as a "hard-core" exception to more liberal treatment, and their trade legislation is well supplied with escape clauses to assure the continuation of restrictive import policies in that sector.

This problem, which will be further explored in Chapter 7, is bound to lead to increasing friction and frustration within the free world as the low-income countries industrialize unless the high-income countries are able radically to alter their point of view. It is a problem demanding more creative policies than any now in evidence if the non-Communist world is to deal adequately with the economic difficulties and aspirations of its poorer members.

The European Community and the Trade Expansion Act

In the realm of policy the American response to the Common Market has been the justly hailed Trade Expansion Act of 1962, which offers a courageous new approach to the subject of trade barriers. Instead of negotiating tariff reductions on a commodity-by-commodity basis, as under the earlier Reciprocal Trade Agreements program, the new legislation authorizes the President to negotiate trade agreements in which, in exchange for reciprocal reductions, tariff cuts can be offered on broad commodity categories. It is a procedure which will not only save a great deal of time and bickering but which—if other countries, and particularly the Community, mean business—should achieve much more significant results. In some cases, as on certain tropical products and on commodities where the duty is five per cent or less, the President will have the authority in such agreements to remove tariffs entirely, but in most cases the authority will be limited to tariff reductions of up to half the duty prevailing on July 1, 1962.[1] As under the earlier programs, tariff reductions offered to one country or to the Community will automatically be extended, under the most-favored-nation clause, to other countries.

The Trade Expansion Act was proposed and enacted mainly in an effort to persuade the emerging Common Market to pursue liberal "outward-looking" trade policies. Whether this will be the result remains to be seen. The premise that the Community, in exchange for major and comprehensive American tariff reductions, will be willing to make correspondingly drastic reductions in its own external duties is currently being tested in the "Kennedy round" of tariff negotiations under the General Agreement on Tariffs and Trade. If that premise—which appears somewhat less plausible in the middle of 1964 than it did in 1962—should not be vindicated, the United States, assuming that it still wishes to make progress toward freer trade, will be confronted with a decision of great importance. Either, on the one hand, it will have to abandon its traditional emphasis on reciprocity in removing trade restrictions or, on the other hand, it will have to abandon, or reinterpret, that other cornerstone of American trade policy: the most-favored-nation clause. This basic question,

[1] The President is also authorized to reduce tariffs to zero on those commodities where the United States and the Common Market countries together account for 80 per cent or more of the value of world exports. This provision would have been of great importance if, as was expected when the legislation was enacted, the United Kingdom were to be added to the Community; without Britain, however, the products covered by the provision are few and unimportant.

15

which here can only be stated, will be among those examined in the final chapter.

We have now surveyed the main issues with which this volume will be concerned. Before proceeding to a systematic analysis, it will be helpful to review briefly the developments leading to the present phase of European integration. To this task we now turn.

2

An Old Dream in a New Form

We hope to reach again a Europe purged of the slavery of ancient days in which men will be as proud to say "I am a European" as once they were to say *"Civis Romanus sum."* We hope to see a Europe where men of every country will think as much of being a European as of belonging to their native land, and wherever they go in this wide domain will truly feel "Here I am at home."

WINSTON CHURCHILL, 1947

The vision of a united Europe, which even a skeptical De Gaulle has called "the dream of the wise,"[1] is a very old dream that has been associated with such illustrious names as Erasmus, Thomas More, Sully, Grotius, William Penn, Leibniz, Kant, and Victor Hugo. The dream has not only varied widely in content and meaning for different dreamers, but has also undergone considerable evolution with the passage of time. Until the twentieth century, the idea of European union was pre-eminently a political aspiration, mainly inspired, in its more idealistic manifestations, by the hope of putting an end to European military strife and political oppression. Thus in 1834, Mazzini offered the statutes of his "Young Europe"; in 1837, the German jurist, Sartorius, proposed a league of European states patterned after the German confederation; and in 1848, a year of revolution and political

---

[1] He added: "and the ambition of the powerful."

17

upheaval, the Italian social philosopher, Carlo Cattaneo, wrote: "We shall have peace when we have a United States of Europe."

Until the First World War such views, although linked to some of the greatest names in history, had little influence outside intellectual circles. Moreover, they had little economic content. The emphasis on economic integration, which is so prominent a feature of European unification in our day, was not a characteristic of earlier thinking on the subject. This is partly because the forces of economic integration, as they revealed themselves during the late eighteenth and all of the nineteenth centuries, operated on a global rather than on a regional scale. The message of Adam Smith and of Cobden and Bright was to remove barriers to the flow of goods and of capital not merely within Europe, but with the whole world. On this basis Britain moved to free trade during the nineteenth century and, while other countries did not move that far, customs duties (which in many countries were mainly for revenue rather than for protection) remained the sole governmental barrier to international trade. Yet to be invented were the much more effective quantitative and exchange restrictions that have been so extensively employed during the past three decades. During the half century preceding the First World War, moreover, most European countries were on the gold standard, which, whatever its flaws, in effect created a common monetary system by providing a regime in which currencies could be freely converted into one another at virtually fixed exchange rates. Thus it is easy to forget that the Europe of sixty or even a hundred years ago had attained a degree of economic integration which in certain respects greatly exceeded that prevailing during most of the years since 1930. Indeed, postwar efforts toward European economic integration have thus far succeeded mainly in eliminating the economic *disintegration* bequeathed by two world wars and the intervening world depression. But this in itself has been a monumental achievement.

Interwar Hopes and Failures

Inevitably, the traumatic impact of the First World War led to a new interest in European union. Shortly after the end of the war the distinguished Italian economist and political leader, Luigi Einaudi, wrote a series of articles advocating a European federation. At about the same time a young Austrian aristocrat, Count Coudenhove-Kalergi, came to the conclusion that only through economic and political unification could Europe avoid a second world war. He formed a movement called Pan-Europe, to which he devoted his life. While his influence was mainly on intellectuals, the Count in 1929 encouraged Briand, then French foreign minister, to propose to the League of Nations a political confederation of Europe which, on the economic side, might assume the form of a customs union. This proposal, which was supported by Streseman, Herriot, and other European leaders, proved to be sadly ill-timed. Streseman, whose powerful influence would have been badly needed if anything were to be achieved, died later in 1929 at the outbreak of the world economic depression.

With the depression, all hope for an early move toward European union abruptly disappeared. Instead of seeking salvation along the path of economic and political integration, Europe quickly yielded to the easier but self-defeating alternative of economic nationalism, which revived on a scale unknown since the days of mercantilism. In an effort to cope with balance-of-payments difficulties resulting from declining exports and the flight of capital, European countries resorted to import quotas and exchange restrictions which, as a by-product, provided a drastic increase in protection from foreign competition.

These developments were carried to their logical limits by the Second World War. Indeed, to what remained of normal international commercial and financial arrangements, the war delivered the *coup de grâce*. In order to conserve gold and foreign currencies (notably dollars) direct controls over trade and payments were greatly extended and, for the same reason, European currencies ceased to be convertible except at administrative discretion. Such trade as took place was carried on mainly by government agencies.

Foundations of Postwar European Cooperation

Thus the prospects for European integration perhaps never appeared less promising than at the end of World War II. Yet, with the advantage of hindsight, it is possible to discern that the time was ripe for a reversal of the disastrous trend that had prevailed since 1929. First, the bitter consequences of depression and war had demonstrated anew the utter futility of dealing with European problems on a basis of uninhibited national sovereignty. Twice in a generation the excesses of European nationalism had led to world conflict; and the intervening depression, far from yielding to policies of economic nationalism, had instead been thereby greatly intensified. In these circumstances it did not take great insight to recognize that any hope for a brighter future lay along another route.

In the second place, the early postwar emergence of Soviet imperialism as the real threat to future peace provided a strong political motive for greater European unity. This development placed West Germany and the rest of Western Europe in the same camp and greatly facilitated that Franco-German cooperation which has played so important a role since 1950. At the same time, the partition of Germany and the Soviet domination of the satellite countries reduced the geographical scope of any moves toward European integration by confining them to Western Europe.

Third, and equally important, the pressure of economic and political events led the United States at an early stage actively to support Western European integration. In the first postwar years the economic devastation inflicted by the war had been woefully underestimated, and there was grave danger that, unless European economic conditions rapidly improved, the numerically strong Communist parties in such countries as France and Italy might come into power—quite possibly by legal means. After uncoordinated and inadequate efforts to promote European revival on a country-by-country basis, the American administration, reacting pragmatically to the logic of events, conceived the Marshall Plan, which was a bold attempt to deal with European problems on a European scale. The great virtue of the new approach was that it required European countries to cooperate closely with one another and, for a time at least, to think primarily in European rather than in national terms. One of the conditions of the assistance provided under the plan was that European governments should jointly formulate a program of economic recovery and— more significantly—should jointly decide, among other things, how the American assistance was to be divided among themselves.

To implement these objectives, the participating countries formed the Organization for European Economic Cooperation (OEEC), which at once became a remarkably effective international institution. From the standpoint of economic integration, its most significant achievements were in the sphere of trade and payments. Even before the OEEC was formed, the European committee which preceded it had given consideration to the possibility of forming a Western European customs union under which tariffs within the area formed by the Marshall Plan countries would disappear. It was widely felt, however, that there would be little point in taking action on tariffs until progress was made in the removal of the much more serious obstacle to intra-European trade presented by quantitative restrictions. Accordingly, the OEEC directed its attention to the more immediate and more pressing objective.

This was no easy task. Quantitative restrictions, as we have seen, emerged during the depression in response to the need to balance international accounts at a time when exports were declining. In the depression years the problem for most countries was merely a problem of achieving an *over-all* balance in external accounts since the major currencies, such as sterling, were still convertible. With the outbreak of the Second World War, however, sterling and other European currencies became inconvertible because of the need to conserve gold and dollars, and, except for a disastrous experiment with sterling convertibility in the summer of 1947, they remained inconvertible during the early postwar years. Moreover, they were inconvertible not only into dollars, but also into one another. Consequently, European trade after the war was able to revive only on the basis of bilateral agreements. In these circumstances the problem for European countries was to achieve not merely a global balance in international accounts but a high degree of bilateral balance as well. To attain such a balance import quotas were extensively employed, and these tended to vary with the requirements of each bilateral position. Thus, in the early postwar years European countries made no effort to apply quotas in a nondiscriminatory manner. On the contrary, discrimination in this sphere flourished toward the outside world as well as within Europe.

Attack on Intra-European Quantitative Restrictions

The task of removing quantitative restrictions within Europe was therefore a highly formidable undertaking, and until 1950 the OEEC made little progress in this direction. As late as October 1949, only 30 per cent of intra-European (intra-OEEC) trade was free from quantitative restrictions, and much of this freedom was on a basis which discriminated within Europe, with freedom accorded to certain OEEC countries but not to others. In that month, Paul G. Hoffman, the American administrator of the

Marshall Plan, made a speech in Paris to the OEEC Council reflecting his conviction that the OEEC should make a frontal attack on trade restrictions within Europe. Declaring that the "economic integration" of Western Europe was a "vital objective" of American policy, Hoffman explained that by economic integration he meant "the formation of a single large market within which quantitative restrictions on the movements of goods, monetary barriers to the flow of payments and, eventually, all tariffs are permanently swept away."[2] The blessing thus given to the cause of European integration by a high American official greatly encouraged European leaders who had reached the same conclusion.

Hoffman gave top priority to the removal of quantitative restrictions, where progress, as we have seen, required an effective attack on bilateralism and inconvertibility within Europe. Such an attack was forthcoming in the form of a remarkably successful and ingenious transitional institution, the European Payments Union (EPU), which was negotiated during the first half of 1950. The EPU, which functioned from September 1950 until the end of 1958, was an arrangement among Western European central banks which provided, in effect, for the inter-convertibility of Western European (OEEC) currencies. This arrangement removed all pressure to achieve bilateral balance within Western Europe and eliminated the financial basis for intra-European commercial discrimination. Moreover, the Union provided each member country with generous drawing rights that were automatically available for the financing of balance-of-payments deficits within the EPU area. The primary immediate purpose of these credit facilities was to encourage OEEC countries rapidly to remove their intra-European import quotas.

In this purpose the EPU, under OEEC direction, was notably

[2] *The New York Times*, November 1, 1949.

successful. By the end of 1950, after only three months of EPU operation, 60 per cent of intra-European trade had been freed from quantitative restrictions; and, in response to a rule of the new OEEC Trade Code, all such freedom was made non-discriminatory—i.e., it was extended to all OEEC countries. After 1950, despite occasional setbacks, this progress continued. Such countries as Italy, Switzerland, and the Benelux group were able to remove almost all their intra-European trade quotas at an early stage after the formation of the Union. Progress in other cases was less dramatic, but by the beginning of 1960, twelve OEEC countries had removed 90 per cent or more of their import quotas on intra-European trade; apart from the countries just mentioned, the list included Austria, France, Germany, Ireland, Portugal, Sweden, and the United Kingdom. In view of the initial difficulties this was a notable achievement—an achievement that virtually removed one of the worst economic legacies of depression and war.[3]

Renewal of Interest in Tariff Problems

On tariffs the record of the OEEC was very different, and developments in this area have taken place mainly under other auspices. Although, from the outset, tariff matters were discussed within the OEEC, and although formal proposals for tariff reduction were from time to time presented to the organization,[4] action in this sphere in the early years was widely regarded as a secondary objective until progress had been made in the removal of import quotas. Hoffman, in his speech on European integration, had

[3] For an excellent early treatment of this subject, see William Diebold, Jr., *Trade and Payments in Western Europe: A Study in Economic Cooperation, 1947-51* (New York: Harper, 1952). For a later authoritative study, see Robert Triffin, *Europe and the Money Muddle: From Bilateralism to Near-convertibility, 1947-56* (New Haven: Yale University Press, 1957).

[4] For a discussion of such proposals, see Diebold, cited, Chapters 11 and 12.

supported the removal, "eventually," of tariffs within Western Europe, but he clearly regarded quantitative restrictions as the immediate problem.

With the dramatic progress in the removal of import quotas which followed the establishment of the European Payments Union, tariffs began to attract greater attention. From a position of second place as a trade obstacle, tariffs (as had been predicted) gradually reacquired their traditional position as the major artificial barrier to international trade. First to be concerned about this change of events were the low-tariff countries, such as Denmark and Switzerland, which felt that by removing quotas they were giving to other OEEC countries a far greater market advantage than were such countries as Italy and France which, because of their high tariffs, would be difficult markets to enter even if all their quotas were eliminated. Thus, from 1950 on, the low-tariff countries increasingly appealed to the OEEC to exert its leadership in getting tariffs down, and in some cases they delayed the removal of their quotas in an effort to spur action.

For the OEEC, however, action on tariffs posed problems of a character that made action more difficult than on quotas. Most OEEC countries were signatories of the General Agreement on Tariffs and Trade (GATT). This agreement permitted participating countries, for balance-of-payments reasons, to remove quantitative restrictions with some countries while retaining them with others, and on this basis OEEC countries had removed quotas among themselves without at first doing so for outside countries. But the agreement did not permit such discrimination in the matter of tariffs. In this area GATT members were to apply to one another the most-favored-nation principle—that is to say, equal treatment.

Certain exceptions were recognized. Where tariff preferences, such as the British Commonwealth Preference regime, already existed, they were permitted to continue, provided the preferences were not increased. Apart from this exception, which applied to the past, there were two exceptions which permitted future deviations from most-favored-nation treatment. One of these related to customs unions, the other to so-called "free-trade areas." Under Article 24 of GATT, a group of countries could form a customs union within which tariffs would be eliminated, while a common schedule of tariffs would be applied to the outside world. This common tariff wall "and other regulations of commerce" could not be "higher or more restrictive than the general incidence of the duties and regulations of commerce applicable in the constituent territories prior to the formation of such union." Alternatively, a group of countries could form a "free-trade area." As in the case of a customs union this would involve the elimination of tariffs within the group but, instead of applying a common tariff schedule against the outside world, each country would continue to apply its existing schedule of tariffs.

The concept of a free-trade area was new and untried, but customs unions had long been a feature of European commercial arrangements. With the exception of the nineteenth-century German *Zollverein*, however, such unions typically were highly unbalanced associations of only two countries, one of which was usually much larger than the other. Four European customs unions had survived the Second World War, and an agreement to form a new union, Benelux, was made by the governments-in-exile of Belgium, the Netherlands, and Luxembourg while the war was still in progress. Except for Benelux, however, these arrangements (France-Monaco, Italy-San Marino, Switzerland-Lichtenstein, and Belgium-Luxembourg), involving the union of a single major European country with a very small country or principality, were of importance only to the smaller partner. Benelux was a different matter, involving the amalgamation of the Netherlands and the Belgium-Luxembourg union. But since the conditions, problems, and policies of the two major countries were often in sharp contrast, Benelux during its first years was so beset with difficulties that it provided little encouragement for bolder projects of the same nature.

The OEEC could, of course, have sponsored a Western European customs union and, as we have seen, consideration had been given to this possibility by the European committee which preceded the OEEC. At that time, however, the proposal was generally regarded as premature. Later, the matter was occasionally mentioned within the OEEC, but nothing ever came of it. In part, the reason was that certain OEEC countries, notably the United Kingdom, relished neither the prospect of becoming a member of a European customs union nor the thought of being excluded from a union embracing the other OEEC countries. In any case, by the time sufficient progress in the removal of quotas had been made to justify serious interest in an OEEC customs union, far-reaching events had taken place which took the initiative outside the OEEC.

The Schuman Plan

The first of these developments was the Schuman Plan, which was a remarkably creative attempt to assure a constructive role for German energies in postwar Europe. In May 1950 Robert Schuman, then French Minister of Foreign Affairs, proposed on behalf of the French government that "the entire French-German production of coal and steel be placed under a common High Authority, in an organization open to the other countries of Europe."

By any standards this was a remarkable venture in economic statesmanship. In terms of postwar European evolution, it represented, not a predictable unfolding of earlier tendencies, but a true mutation. From the outset the plan was regarded by its architects as the first step toward much broader objectives embracing the economic and political integration of Western Europe.

This first step was to weld together, at the very center of their industrial life, the two great nations through which European conflict had so long been polarized. In the words of Robert Schuman, "the solidarity in production thus established will make it plain that any war between France and Germany becomes not merely unthinkable but actually impossible."[5]

To achieve such an ambitious objective an international organization of the OEEC type was clearly not adequate. In its decisions the OEEC operated on the unanimity rule. Decisions, it is true, could be made which were supported by fewer than all the members, but in such cases the decisions were binding only on the members that had agreed to them. The OEEC, that is to say, was an organization of sovereign states. Discarding such a procedure as inadequate, the Schuman Plan provided for a supranational authority, with power to make decisions that were binding on member countries.

Any European country was free to join the arrangement, provided it was willing to accept the terms. In view of the supranational aspects, the United Kingdom chose to remain on the outside. On the other hand, Italy and the Benelux group were prepared to join France and Germany on the terms set forth, and thus was born "the Six." A treaty was signed by foreign ministers in April 1951 and went into effect in July 1952.

The plan provided for a "common market" in coal and steel, in which tariffs and quantitative restrictions within the Six were to be eliminated, not after a long transition period, but almost immediately. For coal, iron ore, and scrap, the common market became effective in February 1953; for steel, it became effective in May 1953.[6] Since the common market was confined to a restricted

[5] *The Times* (London), May 10, 1950, p. 6.
[6] The effective date for special steels was August 1954. For a comprehensive and distinguished study of the Schuman Plan, see William Diebold, Jr., *The Schuman Plan: A Study in Economic Cooperation, 1950-1959* (New York: Praeger, 1959).

group of products—albeit a highly important group—it did not conform to GATT standards, which stipulate that a customs union or free-trade area should apply to "substantially all" trade among the constituent countries. The arrangement therefore required a special dispensation in the form of a GATT waiver. This was granted in November 1952.

If for no other reason, the Schuman Plan was of major significance in giving birth to the Six. With France and Germany as the nucleus, the Six was a group of nations, all of which had suffered either occupation or defeat in World War II. Each had witnessed a tragic demonstration of the inadequacy of dealing with regional or global problems on a national basis, and each was prepared to move faster and further toward economic integration than were the other OEEC countries. Indeed, the three countries of the Benelux group were already in the process of achieving economic integration among themselves.

Plans for a Common Market of the Six

It was natural for the Six, having attained a common market in coal and steel, to extend their horizon to broader objectives. There were some who felt that future evolution might best take place on a sector-by-sector basis. Under this conception a common market in coal and steel would be followed by the successive introduction of common markets in other sectors of production. Except in the field of atomic energy, however, where action was taken on a sectoral basis, the Six eventually decided on a more ambitious objective—namely, a Common Market embracing all commodities.

For a time progress within the Six was limited to implementation of the Schuman Plan. Indeed, the strong feelings aroused by the French failure in 1954 to ratify the agreement for a European Defense Community led to speculation that the Six might not have sufficient cohesion to undertake any new initiatives toward economic integration. Such speculation, however, proved unduly pessimistic. As early as June 1955 the foreign ministers of the Six at a meeting in Messina agreed that joint action should be taken in the field of atomic energy, and "cautiously endorsed," as a more distant objective, a general Common Market.[7]

For the time being, a common market in atomic energy—"Euratom"—seemed the more realistic and more readily attainable objective, but the Six soon made it clear that they were also serious in their intention to establish a Common Market for all production. After months of discussion in the latter part of 1955 and in early 1956, during which many troublesome issues were provisionally settled, the foreign ministers of the Six in May 1956 agreed at a meeting in Venice that the time had come to begin drafting treaties both for Euratom and for a general Common Market.

By a Common Market, the Six did not mean simply a customs union. A customs union was an essential aspect of a common market, and by itself would have been a bold step forward, but the Six were convinced that even bolder action was necessary if lasting progress were to be achieved. Leaders of the Six indicated that their goal was a genuine economic union in which, in addition to regional free trade in commodities, there would be free movement of labor and capital, freedom to establish enterprises anywhere within the union, and—perhaps most important of all —a coordination of economic policy, particularly in the monetary and fiscal fields. They were convinced that such coordination was necessary to assure both that the interests of all member countries would be adequately safeguarded and that the arrangement would have sufficient vitality to survive the rough shocks which might

[7] A brief account of these developments is provided in Miriam Camps, *The European Common Market and American Policy* (Princeton: Center of International Studies, 1956).

30

from time to time be expected in a rapidly changing world. The Six therefore decided, as in the case of the Schuman Plan, to set up supranational institutions with the authority, by qualified majority vote, to make decisions which would be binding on all member countries.

The Six made one decision, however, that was in sharp contrast to the provisions of the Schuman Plan. That plan had virtually dispensed with a transition period for the attainment of its objectives; as we have seen, tariffs and quantitative restrictions within the Six on the affected products were removed almost immediately. For the much more ambitious objective of establishing a common market embracing all production, the Six decided that such a time schedule would be far too abrupt. Accordingly, they agreed that the new arrangement should be gradually established over a transition period of twelve years—a period which could subsequently be lengthened or shortened if conditions warranted.

Events during 1956 and 1957 moved rapidly. The Suez crisis, which during late 1956 and early 1957 provided another painful lesson of the dangers of uncoordinated national action, spurred the Six in their collective endeavors. In March 1957 foreign ministers of the Six signed a treaty in Rome establishing the Common Market, to be known as the "European Economic Community." During the remaining months of 1957 the treaty was ratified by the participating governments, and formally went into effect on January 1, 1958.

Central Provisions of the Rome Treaty

The Rome Treaty is a long document; in English translation, its 248 articles, together with the appended annexes, protocols, conventions, and declarations, comprise a book of 378 pages. The main features of the treaty, however, can be summarized fairly briefly.

The purpose of the Community is stated in Article 2. By "establishing a Common Market," the Community seeks to promote "a harmonious development of economic activities, a continuous and balanced expansion, an increased stability, an accelerated raising of the standard of living, and closer relations between the member states." The final phrase hints delicately at aspirations toward political union, yet one can search through the treaty in vain for the word "political." The political aspects of the Community, although important, remain entirely implicit.

While the treaty has nothing to say about political union, even as an aspiration, its provisions go far beyond the establishment simply of a customs union. The clear aim of Article 3 is to provide for a genuine economic union. Thus, in addition to creating a customs union, it calls for the elimination within the Community of "obstacles to the free movement of persons, services, and capital"; the inauguration of a "common agricultural policy" and a "common transport policy"; the "establishment of a system ensuring that competition shall not be distorted in the Common Market"; the "application of procedures . . . to coordinate the economic policies of member states and to remedy disequilibria in their balances of payments"; the creation of a European Social Fund to "improve the possibilities of employment for workers and to contribute to the raising of their standard of living"; the establishment of a European Investment Bank to "facilitate the economic expansion of the Community through the creation of new resources"; and the association with the Community, on a special basis, of the overseas countries and territories affiliated with the Six. Some of the provisions, such as that for a customs union, are either well under way or, as in the case of the European Investment Bank, fully in effect; others, such as the "common agricultural policy" have been the subject of extended controversy, with agreement yet to be reached on major matters. Still others, such as the provision for coordination of economic policies, as yet remain to a large extent within the realm of aspiration.

To implement the treaty, Article 4 establishes four institutions: a Council, a Commission, an Assembly, and a Court of Justice. The Council is a policy-making body of ministerial rank, with one representative from each member state. Its composition varies with the subject matter under consideration. Thus, on agricultural matters the representation would normally consist of Ministers of Agriculture; on transportation matters, Ministers of Transport, and so on. Except where otherwise provided in the treaty, the Council makes its decisions by "qualified" majority vote, in which member votes are weighted roughly according to populations, as follows: France, 4; Germany, 4; Italy, 4; Belgium, 2; the Netherlands, 2; and Luxembourg, 1. To be adopted, decisions require at least twelve votes. Under these rules no single country (nor the Benelux Union operating as a unit) can prevent Council action. On certain matters, such as the admission of new members, the treaty requires unanimous Council decisions; in such instances, however, abstention from voting does not block a decision.

In contrast to the Council, which has made a practice of meeting monthly, the Commission has charge of the day-to-day operations of the Community. The Commission is directed to "ensure the application" of the various provisions of the treaty and of the regulations enacted under the authority of the treaty by the Community's several institutions. In performing this function the Commission is instructed to "formulate recommendations or opinions" for the consideration of the Council on matters covered by the treaty. The Commission consists of nine members, not more than two of whom may be from the same member state. Members are appointed for a renewable four-year term by the participating governments "acting in common agreement."

All decisions of the Commission are made by simple majority vote. In contrast to members of the Council, who in effect are representatives of their respective governments, members of the Commission are specifically forbidden to "seek or accept instructions from any government or other body." They are directed to "perform their duties in the general interest of the Community with complete independence," and member states, on their part, are "not to seek to influence the members of the Commission in the performance of their duties."

The Council and the Commission serve only the European Economic Community. The Assembly (European Parliament) and the Court of Justice, however, serve all three creations of the Six: the European Economic Community, Euratom, and the European Coal and Steel Community. The European Parliament consists of 142 delegates who are at present chosen by the national legislatures. At its first meeting in March 1958 the European Parliament decided to be seated, not as national delegations nor in alphabetical order, but according to political party groupings. The Parliament must be consulted on various matters, including the annual budget, but its most important power is its control over the executive. Under a "motion of censure" the Parliament, by a two-thirds majority, can require the resignation of the entire Commission.

The judicial functions of the Community are performed by the Court of Justice. The Court is composed of seven judges who are appointed by the member governments acting in common agreement. It makes rulings on treaty matters raised by member countries or by institutions of the Community, and functions as a court of final appeal on matters pertaining to the treaty.

The Community's Timetable

As already noted above, the objectives of the Rome Treaty are to be attained over a transition period which, under certain conditions, may be either lengthened or shortened. The transition period was originally conceived to extend from a minimum of twelve to a maximum of fifteen years. During this period internal tariffs and quantitative restrictions were to be gradually removed according to a somewhat flexible timetable, and a common external tariff was to be achieved in a series of steps, the first step not to take place until the end of the first of three four-year "stages" (i.e., not before December 31, 1961).

When the treaty was negotiated, much attention was given to the possibility of lengthening the transition period, and virtually no attention to the possibility of shortening it. Since the treaty has gone into effect, however, the latter possibility has been more evident. In part, this change of outlook has reflected the greatly improved economic position of France, but it has also reflected an increased awareness of the positive advantages of a shorter transition. By its very nature a transition period introduces a situation of uncertainty, in which producers and investors are confronted with conditions which are different both from those prevailing before, and from those prevailing after, the interregnum. By accelerating the transition, this period of uncertainty is reduced, investment decisions are thus easier to make, and the beneficial effects of regional free trade are felt earlier.

Although not expecting the authority to be used, the drafters of the Rome Treaty provided for the possibility of shortening the transition period to less than the contemplated twelve-year minimum. By a unanimous vote, the Council—after consulting the European Parliament and on the basis of a proposal by the Commission—can advance the timetable for internal tariff reduction. The Council also has the power to advance the date for the attainment of the common external tariff and to accelerate the removal of quantitative restrictions. Acting on this authority, the Council in May 1960 decided, as part of an acceleration program proposed by the Commission, that the third internal tariff reduction of ten per cent, originally scheduled for December 31, 1961, should take place not later than January 1, 1961,[8] and that the first step toward the common external tariff should take place on January 1, 1961—one year earlier than originally prescribed.

Acceleration of the Rome Treaty timetable has been particularly noteworthy in the case of quantitative trade barriers. Originally it was contemplated that the removal of import quotas would take place gradually throughout the entire transition period, and rules were established on the basis of this rather relaxed approach. With the rapid reduction of quantitative restrictions following the Western European return to convertibility at the end of 1958, the targets laid down in the Rome Treaty became an anachronism. In view of the progress already achieved, the Council in May 1960 decided, as part of its acceleration program, that member states, in accordance with their GATT obligations, should abolish as soon as possible all import quotas on industrial products, regardless of source. No time limit was set for the removal of quotas on outside products, but the decision provided that quotas on industrial products originating within the Community must be eliminated by the end of 1961.

Both for the Six and for the rest of Western Europe, acceleration of the Community's timetable had a political as well as an economic significance. For the Six, acceleration was regarded as evidence to all—and particularly to other European countries—that the Community had reached the point of no return. For the rest of Western Europe, it is fair to say, acceleration was a totally unexpected and highly disturbing development which played an important part in bringing about a radical change in thinking—particularly in British thinking—about European union.

---

[8] Agricultural products not protected by import quotas were exempted from this speed-up; agricultural products under quota were subject to a five per cent tariff reduction.

3

Toward a United Europe—or a United "Little Europe"?

A few weeks ago, . . . I was asked what I proposed as the "solution" of our problems in Europe. I promised my questioner that while in Greece I would put the problem to the Delphic Oracle. But I added that I knew in advance what the answer would be: "Build a bridge." Indeed, this phrase seems to me the perfect Delphic answer, in that everyone can interpret it as he chooses, but no two people are agreed on what it means.

WALTER HALLSTEIN, 1959

Looking ahead, . . . what we want is a complete Europe, that is to say the unity of the whole of Free Europe. To bring this about while taking into account the particular interests of each country, . . . it is obviously necessary that the initiative of the Six countries be regarded as something which is capable of extension to the rest of Europe.

BARON SNOY ET D'OPPUERS, 1960

For the Western European countries outside the "Little Europe" of the Six, the Common Market, as it began to take shape in the mid-1950s, was a far from reassuring development. For reasons that differed from case to case, these countries did not wish to be members of the union envisaged by the Six, but neither did they wish to suffer from the unfavorable tariff changes for outsiders which such a union would bring into being. Under the prospective customs union German tariffs, for example, on French, Italian, and Benelux products would gradually disappear, while German

37

tariffs against all other countries, including the debarred OEEC countries, would continue in effect. Indeed, since most German tariffs were below the average for the Six as a group, there was the prospect that formation of the common tariff applying to outside products would involve an average increase in German tariffs against the outside world. In the eyes of the OEEC countries outside the Common Market the result of such tariff changes within the Six would mean the reappearance, on a broad scale, of commercial "discrimination" within Western Europe.[1]

In the removal of intra-European quantitative restrictions the OEEC, as we have seen, had adopted a rule of nondiscrimination. The rule had worked well, and had been generally regarded as a major reason for OEEC success in removing quotas since it had eliminated an important source of disharmony. In its Trade Code, the OEEC had conferred its blessing upon the formation of new customs unions, but this blessing had been given with such peripheral developments as Benelux in mind. The possibility of extensive intra-European tariff "discrimination" from a customs union the size of the Common Market was simply not foreseen.

This was not a prospect that the OEEC countries outside the proposed Common Market could take lightly. For almost all such countries the Six were a highly important market. In most cases exports to the prospective Common Market countries accounted for at least one-fourth of total exports, and for some countries the fraction was much higher. For example, about two-fifths of Swiss exports went to the Six, while for Austria the fraction was about

[1] The use of the term "discrimination" in this connection was the source of heated exchanges between the Six and the other OEEC countries. Understandably, the Common Market countries contended that it is unfair to refer to the extension of free trade within a customs union—but not to outsiders—as discrimination, since this is never the practice when speaking of national customs areas. Equally understandably, the other OEEC countries contended that, whatever the tariff changes accompanying the Common Market were called, the effects for them were clearly discriminatory.

one-half. In such circumstances the possibility of tariff changes that might make the Six a much more difficult market to enter was regarded by the excluded OEEC countries as a highly disturbing and unfavorable development.

By the summer of 1956 the avoidance of this unwelcome prospect had become a major objective of the Western European countries outside the Six. How to achieve the objective was a difficult question. One solution would have been to join the proposed Community. But this, for one reason or another, the countries outside were not prepared to do. Switzerland was not prepared to join because it felt that its traditional neutrality would be compromised if it were to be the member of a group that might some day become a political union. Austria, whose neutrality was imposed from without, could not join for the same reason. Sweden also wished to preserve its neutrality and, like the other Scandinavian countries, wished to maintain its close commercial ties with the United Kingdom. For its part, the United Kingdom in 1956 regarded joining the Common Market as out of the question, and it is only fair to add that at the time the possibility of United Kingdom membership would have been at least as unwelcome to one or two of the prospective Common Market countries.

British Proposal for an OEEC Free-Trade Area

As the leading industrial OEEC country outside the Six, however, the United Kingdom soon realized that it would have to assume leadership in any effort to avoid the emergence of intra-European tariff discrimination. Accordingly, the British in July 1956 submitted to the OEEC Council a bold new proposal for a free-trade area which would embrace all OEEC countries and which would include the Six, in effect, as one country. Under this proposal the Six would continue with their plans as scheduled, but would apply

39

their common tariff wall only against non-OEEC countries. Within the OEEC they would gradually remove tariffs according to the schedule originally intended only for Community members and at the end of the transition period would be on a free-trade basis with all OEEC countries. Likewise, Britain and other non-Community OEEC countries would proceed to remove all tariffs (except those on agricultural products) within the OEEC area. Instead of forming a common tariff wall with the outside world, however, these countries would continue to apply their existing tariffs to non-OEEC countries.

The British proposal was ingenious and was carefully designed to achieve a single objective—the avoidance of imminent tariff discrimination between the Six and the other OEEC countries—and to achieve this objective in a way which would not disturb existing Commonwealth arrangements or British agricultural policies. The proposal was strictly limited to the commercial terrain and, as just noted, excluded agricultural products; it had nothing to say about the movement of capital or manpower, the coordination of fiscal or monetary policy, or the establishment of international institutions. It was exclusively addressed to intra-European trade barriers and, in particular, to tariffs. But since tariffs had been discussed within the OEEC for several years in an atmosphere of increasing frustration because nothing had been accomplished, the British proposal was received by the OEEC countries outside the Six with serious interest if not enthusiasm.[2] Accordingly, despite considerable skepticism on the part of the Six with respect to British motives and intentions, the OEEC Council agreed that the organization should study the proposal as a possible basis for future action.

It would not be much of an exaggeration to say that considera-

---

[2] The enthusiasms of such low-tariff countries as Denmark was restrained by the failure of the British to include agricultural products in the proposed free-trade area.

tion of the British proposal was the dominant activity of the OEEC during the next two and a half years. Discussions began in a hopeful atmosphere, and in January 1957 an OEEC committee reported that a free-trade area embracing the OEEC countries, including the Six, was "technically possible." In February the OEEC Council decided that the time had come to begin negotiations for the formation of such a free-trade area, and during the remainder of 1957 discussions within the OEEC proceeded on the assumption that the establishment of a Western European free-trade-area would definitely take place. By the more optimistic, in fact, the objective was regarded as a foregone conclusion, with failure "unthinkable."

At about the beginning of 1958, however, the outlook rapidly changed. On January 1 of that year the Rome Treaty went into effect. It stipulated that the initial tariff reduction within the Six —a reduction of 10 per cent—should take place on January 1, 1959. This meant that if intra-European tariff discrimination were to be completely avoided, agreement on the British proposal would have to be reached by the latter date. Thus January 1, 1959, came to be regarded by the British as a deadline for agreement and, as the date approached, a note of desperation became apparent on the British side. Unfortunately for the British, this feeling of urgency was not shared by the Six. In particular, it was not shared by the French, who by mid-1958 had come to regard their differences with the British as irreconcilable. The discussions increasingly became, as the French put it, a "dialogue of the deaf," and in November 1958 the negotiations collapsed in an atmosphere of great bitterness.

Reasons for Rejection of British Proposal

In retrospect, it is not difficult to understand why negotiations broke down.[3] From the beginning there were a number of serious obstacles to agreement, and these became more difficult to overlook as time went on. First, but not foremost, there were the purely technical difficulties inherent in the new and virtually untried concept of a free-trade area. These difficulties were of particular concern to the French not only because of their long protectionist tradition but because of their persistent balance-of-payments difficulties. Under a free-trade area, as we have seen, each country would retain its tariffs with the outside world, while removing tariffs within the area. In the absence of comprehensive controls such a regime, according to the French, would lead to serious trade "distortion."

Such trade distortion could occur in at least two ways. In the first place, imports (e.g., French imports) from the outside world (e.g., the United States) would tend no longer to come directly to France, where they would be subject to French tariffs (i.e., the common tariff of the Six), but would tend to come via the low-tariff countries (e.g., Denmark) and to enter France disguised as Danish exports which, because allegedly originating from a member of the free-trade area, would be entitled to enter duty-free. In principle such a situation could be avoided by an effective control system based on certificates of origin. Moreover, in the case of readily identifiable products, such as Cadillacs and Royal typewriters, it would be easy for the French authorities to determine the true origin of the imports, regardless of certification.

But this was not the only type of possible trade "distortion" the French had in mind. In addition to products originating outside the European free-trade area, there would be a large group of products which were manufactured inside the area but which were largely or exclusively made from raw materials or semi-manufactured goods imported from the outside world. In some instances only the final stage of production—a stage perhaps

---

[3] For an excellent and more detailed discussion of the free-trade area negotiations and of the reasons for their failure, see Miriam Camps, *The Free Trade Area Negotiations* (London: Political and Economic Planning, 1959).

accounting for only a small percentage of the value of the product —might take place in Europe. In extreme cases, such products to all intents would be outside products, but they presumably would not be listed as outside products under a certificate-of-origin procedure since the trademark or brand name would identify them as European. Yet if such products were regarded as European products, they would be entitled to enter any OEEC country free of duty. If this were permitted, the free-trade-area arrangement would clearly encourage an American exporter, for example, to have the final stage of production take place not in the United States, but in a low-tariff country (e.g., Denmark) inside the free-trade area. He would then be subject only to the low Danish duty for exports which might actually be destined for countries with much higher duties inside the area.

Needless to say, this is not the sort of situation which would worry a classical free trader; but it was a source of real concern to the French, who argued that, without comprehensive safeguards, a free-trade area would reduce their tariffs, in effect, to the level of the country with the lowest tariffs in the area. Moreover, under such conditions any tariff revenue would flow not to France, but to the low-tariff country where the final stage of production took place.

Here was a real dilemma. If *all* goods made inside the area from imported materials were regarded as European goods, and were thus entitled to enter any OEEC country duty-free, effective tariffs would tend to be brought down to the level of the countries with the lowest tariffs (and these countries would receive all the tariff revenues). On the other hand, if *no* goods made inside the area from imported materials were regarded as European goods, the arrangement would be confined to only a small fraction of European production—i.e., to products containing no outside materials. In the first case the arrangement would be much too liberal to be acceptable to the high-tariff countries, while in the second case the arrangement would be of such limited scope as to be of little practical interest.

The British and other advocates of the free-trade area were of course aware of this problem. They proposed a compromise. Products should be regarded as European products if an agreed percentage (say, 50 per cent) or more of their value were of purely European origin.[4] Otherwise, they should be regarded as outside products. This was clearly a possible solution to the problem, but it was not a solution which completely satisfied the critics of a free-trade area. To determine the percentage of value added in Europe would not always be easy, even in principle, and might give rise to much controversy and litigation in doubtful cases. Moreover, effective enforcement might involve a considerable expansion of the customs bureaucracy.

It would be a serious misreading of events, however, to assume that the objections of France and other members of the Six to the British proposal were exclusively technical in character. Moreover, it would be an over-simplification to assume that the objections of the Six were almost exclusively French. The French views on the free-trade area were almost invariably shared by the Italians, and on some central issues they were shared by the German and Benelux leadership as well.

From the outset there was a profound difference between the economic philosophy of the Six, as reflected in the idea of a Common Market, and the economic philosophy of the British, as reflected in the idea of a free-trade area. Both sides, it is true, favored regional free trade. But the architects of the Common Market were convinced that, to make regional free trade work, it was necessary not only to have a common tariff (which would

[4] Alternatively, the British proposed that certain agreed types of processing within Europe might confer European status to products made from outside materials, regardless of the percentage of total value accounted for by such materials.

obviate all the technical difficulties discussed above) but also to have a comprehensive coordination of economic policies under the direction and control of supranational institutions. The British, on the other hand, felt that regional free trade could be made to work not only without a coordination of economic policies, but even without a common tariff.

But the difference in outlook went much deeper than this. The Six regarded regional free trade not as an end in itself but as a means to much broader objectives—that is to say, as a means to economic (and ultimately to political) union. In sharp contrast, the aims of the British, far from being broader than regional free trade, were actually much narrower. The British became interested in regional free trade in 1956 only because they wished to remove the threat of intra-European tariff discrimination. In other words, the free-trade-area proposal was a somewhat tardy response to the plans of the Six, and did not reflect an interest in regional free trade as such. If it had been possible to avoid tariff discrimination without removing intra-European tariffs, the British would have preferred to leave tariffs where they were, but the plans of the Six appeared to rule out the easier course.

Given the basic difference in outlook between the Six and the British, it is hardly surprising that many within the Six, particularly the French, were deeply suspicious of British motives in sponsoring the free-trade-area proposal. The British, these observers believed, were trying to undermine, or in any case dilute, the efforts of the Six toward greater union. Even Raymond Aron, the distinguished French political essayist, has referred to the British proposal as a device "which the French saw simply as an attempt to torpedo the Common Market, and I can hardly see what other purpose they could have read into it."[5]

Whether such views were fair to the British (and they surely

[5] *The Observer*, London, April 3, 1960, p. 21.

were not entirely fair), they did not provide an atmosphere conducive to successful negotiation. Nevertheless, even if the French had not had any doubts about the purity of British motives, they would have found it very difficult in 1958 to accept the British proposal; moreover, this would have been true even if the OEEC countries outside the Six had been prepared to accept a common tariff instead of insisting on a free-trade area. For, what the French found exceedingly uncongenial was the prospect of increasing the area of competition. It had been a great strain for France in 1957 to accept the idea of removing tariffs within the Six; it proved to be simply beyond French capacity to accept participation in a much broader market in which France would be exposed, in particular, to British competition as well as to its formidable competitors within the European Economic Community.

From this standpoint the free-trade area negotiations could hardly have taken place at a less auspicious time. For centuries France had been a stronghold of protectionism, but in the postwar years French trade barriers had been maintained not so much through choice as through necessity. In the years following the 1949 devaluations France had been less successful than most of its neighbors in curbing inflationary tendencies and as a result became increasingly uncompetitive, particularly in relation to Germany, but also in relation to the rest of Europe. This unfortunate trend led inevitably to persistent balance-of-payments difficulties which tended to drain French reserves of gold and dollars. Highly reluctant to devalue, France relied heavily on quantitative restrictions to maintain a tolerable degree of external balance. Early in 1957 the balance-of-payments situation became so serious that France, which had chronically encountered difficulty meeting the minimum OEEC targets of trade liberalization, resorted to an escape clause in the OEEC Trade Code and reimposed quantitative restrictions on all of its intra-European trade. (Its extra-European trade was, of course, already under stringent quota regulation.) Thus, quite apart from the increasingly serious political situation which came to a head in the constitutional crisis of 1958, France was in no mood to undertake obligations which over a period of years would have increased the area of competition greatly beyond that already reluctantly agreed to when France ratified the Rome Treaty.

Developments at the End of 1958

The collapse of the free-trade-area negotiations was shortly followed by three important events which took place almost simultaneously. Perhaps the most significant of these was the unexpected OEEC decision at the end of 1958 to terminate the European Payments Union and to invoke the European Monetary Agreement of 1955. The European Monetary Agreement provided for a return to "market convertibility" of the major Western European currencies. In the early 1950s, foreign-exchange markets along traditional lines had been re-established in the leading European financial centers, but the dollar could not be bought or sold in these markets.[6] The European Monetary Agreement removed this limitation. Henceforward French francs, for example, could be exchanged for dollars as well as for sterling, deutsche marks, and other OEEC currencies.

The return to convertibility removed the financial incentive for European commercial discrimination against the outside world. Under the new regime a Danish deficit with the United States was no more difficult to finance than a Danish deficit with France,

[6] Sterling, however, had by 1955 achieved a form of *de facto* convertibility in certain financial centers; but since this convertibility rested on no formal commitments, it did not provide a solid basis for a return to nondiscriminatory commercial policies. This matter is discussed further in the author's monograph, *Toward European Convertibility*, Essays in International Finance, No. 31, International Finance Section, Princeton University, November 1958.

since francs and dollars were interchangeable. As the more thoughtful were quick to realize, this new situation (or, rather, this return to an old situation) had far-reaching implications, and inevitably altered the perspective on European regional developments. In particular it raised the question whether, in the absence of aspirations toward political union or of other noncommercial objectives, a regional approach to the removal of European trade barriers (as embodied, for example, in the free-trade-area proposal) was any longer justified.

A second important development which occurred at the end of 1958 was the devaluation of the French franc. As 1959 approached it became abundantly clear that France, because of its grave balance-of-payments difficulties, would not be able to comply with its initial obligations under the Rome Treaty unless drastic financial reforms were put into effect. At the eleventh hour such action was forthcoming. With great courage the French authorities not only devalued the franc[7] but, without resorting to escape clauses, immediately accepted all their responsibilities under the European Monetary Agreement, the OEEC Trade Code, and the Rome Treaty. Their judgment proved to be abundantly vindicated. Notwithstanding the return to convertibility with the dollar and despite the extensive removal of quantitative restrictions both within Europe and with the outside world, French holdings of gold and dollars almost doubled in nine months, climbing from $1.1 billion as of December 31, 1958, to $2.0 billion as of September 30, 1959.

Finally, as provided in the Rome Treaty, the European Eco-

---

[7] A partial devaluation of the franc, which took the form of a 20 per cent tax on most imports and a 20 per cent subsidy to exports, had previously taken place in the summer of 1957. This devaluation was very limited in its effects, however, since the new regime simply replaced an exceedingly cumbersome system of import taxes and export subsidies. Moreover, the new import taxes for a time did not apply to certain important commodities, such as coal.

nomic Community on January 1, 1959, put into effect its initial internal tariff reduction of 10 per cent. To soften the blow, the Six decided that this first tariff reduction should be extended to all GATT countries in those cases where such action would not bring duties below the projected common tariff of the Community.[8] This meant that most tariff reductions of the high-tariff countries of the Six (France and Italy) were extended to the United States and other GATT countries outside the Community, whereas most tariff reductions of the low-tariff countries (Germany and the Benelux group) were not generalized.

The European Free Trade Association

Having failed in their initial purpose of establishing a free-trade area embracing all OEEC countries, the United Kingdom and six other OEEC members (the three Scandinavian countries, neutral Austria and Switzerland, and Portugal) reached agreement during 1959 on an alternative objective: the formation of a free-trade area among themselves. A treaty establishing a European Free Trade Association (EFTA) was signed by ministers in January 1960, and was soon ratified by the participating governments. It went into effect on May 3, 1960.[9]

The Association has a combined population slightly more than half that of the Six. Within the Association tariffs are being reduced according to a timetable which is closely adjusted to that of the European Economic Community. Like the Community, the Association is ahead of schedule, and by the end of 1963 had reduced internal tariffs by 60 per cent. As a free-trade area, the Association will not have a common external tariff; customs

[8] In the form taken, this action merely accelerated a situation which would have eventually been required under the Rome Treaty.

[9] In March 1961 Finland became associatd with EFTA on a special basis which confers most of the rights and obligations applying to the original members.

duties applying to the outside world will remain under the control of the individual members. In other respects the Association follows closely the original British proposal for an OEEC free-trade area. Thus the internal tariff reductions do not apply to agricultural products, although special arrangements have been made for certain agricultural commodities. Likewise, the rules for determining which products will receive "area treatment" (i.e., will be entitled to the internal tariff reductions) are patterned closely after the rules which the British had originally proposed for an OEEC free-trade arrangement.[10]

The decision of the Seven to form a free-trade area among themselves was in no way surprising. As they were the first to admit, their primary reason for uniting was to improve their prospects for obtaining a broader free-trade setup which in some way would include the Six. For a time, indeed, many within the Association continued to hope that, in spite of the breakdown of negotiations at the end of 1958, agreement would eventually be reached on a Western European regional free-trade system along the lines of the 1956 British proposal.

British Bid for Membership in the Common Market

By mid-1960, however, such hopes had all but disappeared, and in the second half of the year the British began actively to consider other possibilities. In February 1961 they indicated that they were prepared to explore some form of association with the European Economic Community. At this stage they were not thinking

[10] Thus there are three ways in which imported products can qualify for area treatment: (1) if they have been wholly produced within the Association; (2) if they have been produced within the Association and the value of non-area materials in their manufacture does not exceed 50 per cent; and (3) if they have been produced within the Association by certain specified processes. As an example of the last method of qualification, phonograph records stamped within the Association are entitled to area treatment even if the value of non-area materials in their manufacture exceeds 50 per cent.

in terms of becoming full members, but rather were interested in forming a purely commercial link with the Six. More specifically, the British revealed that they would be prepared to consider a "harmonized" common tariff encircling both the United Kingdom and the Community. They stipulated, however, that the United Kingdom should not be required to apply the common tariff either to its partners in the Commonwealth or to its partners in the European Free Trade Association. Moreover, as in their earlier proposals, they excluded agricultural products from the suggested arrangement.

During the early months of 1961 the British had bilateral talks with members of the Community in an effort to determine the feasibility of such a form of association. By mid-year, however, it became evident that the British government was contemplating a much bolder step—namely, application for full membership in the Community—a step for which it obtained parliamentary approval on August 3. Chapter 6 examines this important subject more thoroughly.

There were several reasons for this bolder approach. For one thing it was clear from the outset that a British proposal for association with the Community that was limited to the commercial terrain would meet with a decidedly unenthusiastic reception from the French. At the same time it was also clear that, in view of President de Gaulle's somewhat contemptuous attitude toward "supra-national" institutions,[11] the British would have little to

---

[11] On more than one occasion De Gaulle has made his views on "supra-nationalism" quite clear. At a press conference in Paris on September 5, 1960, after giving his blessing to the goal of European union, he declared: "Admittedly, as a provisional measure, we have been able to set up a number of more or less supra-national bodies; these bodies have their technical value but they have not, and cannot have, any political authority.... As long as nothing serious happens, they function fairly well without too much trouble, but as soon as something dramatic happens and a serious problem has to be settled, it can be seen that no High Authority has political authority: it is only the states which have it." (Quoted in the PEP pamphlet, *France and the European Economic Community*, January 1961, p. 10.)

fear, for the time being, from the political evolution of the Community. In any case, it was evident that as a member the United Kingdom would be in a position to influence the Community's political development. Perhaps the most important consideration in the British decision to apply for membership was the hope that by sharing in the Community's rapid economic growth the United Kingdom would be able to deal more effectively with its own serious economic problems. In this connection, it was not wholly a coincidence that the British decision came during a crisis in the balance of payments. Finally, and of great significance, the British government, in its bid for membership in the Community, had the strong encouragement of the new American administration.

4

Integration and European Economic Strength

If the countries of Europe do not have the same weight in the world economy as the United States or the Soviet Union, it is to their divisions that they owe this. The creation of a great internal market is indispensable to give Europeans the possibility of retrieving their position and of playing their role in the progress of the free world.

JEAN MONNET, 1953

From the standpoint of American security in a cold war world, the paramount economic question which the Common Market raises for the United States is its impact, particularly in the longer run, on Atlantic economic strength—that is to say, its effect, first of all, on the economic strength of Western Europe and, equally important, its effect on the economic strength of the United States. The first of these matters, the economic impact of the Common Market on Western Europe, is the subject of the present chapter.[1]

Since the Common Market, from an economic point of view, is an effort to achieve regional (but not global) free trade, the question with which we are concerned in this chapter may be rephrased as follows: How does the removal of trade barriers within a large section of Western Europe affect European economic strength, as reflected in such variables as real income per capita, output per

[1] The impact of the Common Market on the American economy is considered in Chapter 8.

53

man-hour, and the rate of economic growth? Economically, the Common Market is of course more than simply a move toward regional free trade. But most of the other economic objectives—for example, the free movement of labor and capital, the common transport policy, and the coordination of fiscal and monetary policy—may be thought of as efforts to assure the desired economic gains from the wider market made possible by the removal of tariffs within the Community. Thus the central question that needs to be examined in this connection is the economic case for a regional attack on trade barriers.

Until the mid-1950s it was possible, in the case of Western Europe, to justify such an attack along two entirely distinct lines of reasoning. First, one could make a purely financial case based on European weakness, as reflected in the closely related conditions of dollar shortage, inadequate monetary reserves, and currency inconvertibility. Second, one could make a broadly economic case—a case which, with certain qualifications, would follow closely the familiar argumentation for global free trade.

Of these two lines of reasoning, the second remains unaffected by the events of recent years. The same cannot be said, however, of the first. Indeed, the financial case has gradually but completely disappeared. Yet it was the financial case which in the early postwar years impelled Western Europe toward a strictly regional attack on trade barriers. These financial conditions have changed so profoundly—and, to many observers, so unexpectedly—that a brief review is in order before turning to the more interesting positive economic case for free trade within Western Europe.

The Financial Case for a Regional Approach in Western Europe

Under the conditions prevailing in the early postwar years, the financial case for a regional rather than a global attack on European trade barriers was very strong. In a situation of acute international disequilibrium focused on the United States, it was possible to make much more rapid progress in the reduction of barriers to intra-European trade than in the reduction of barriers to European trade with the outside world. In practical terms, the alternative to a regional attack on trade barriers was not a global attack, but no attack at all. Wisely, Western Europe chose to make progress where progress could be made, and on this basis succeeded during the early 1950s in removing the bulk of its intra-European import quotas. For the time being, this action was accompanied by virtually no progress in reducing the exceedingly tight restrictions on European purchases from the Dollar Area.

This regional attack on trade barriers was confined to quantitative restrictions. For countries belonging to the International Monetary Fund and participating in the General Agreement on Tariffs and Trade, the legal basis for the resulting commercial discrimination against the outside world rested on payments grounds, and thus received only temporary authorization.[2] Nevertheless, there were many in 1950 who doubted that the financial conditions responsible for the discrimination would, in fact, be temporary. This was the period of acute dollar shortage and a time when the economic journals were full of pessimistic discussions of the "world dollar problem." Some economists on both sides of the Atlantic were not content to explain the situation in terms of the economic damage inflicted by the Second World War, but were inclined to regard the dollar problem as more or less permanent in character, the result of an unusual combination of chronic conditions.

Perhaps the strongest statement of this position was made as recently as April 1957. In a lecture delivered at the Harvard Graduate School of Business Administration, Sir Geoffrey Crowther, former editor of *The Economist*, declared that the dollar problem

[2] Under Article XIV of the Fund Agreement and under Article XIV of the General Agreement on Tariffs and Trade.

55

was "a situation without any precedent, or even an approach to a precedent, in economic history. . . . It is difficult to believe that there can ever have been another case of a country where the demand of the rest of the world for its products was so urgent, and its demand for the products of the rest of the world so indifferent—where rises in price would choke off so few sales on the one side and falls in price stimulate so few purchases on the other —as is the case with the United States today."[3] From this reasoning he drew the conclusion that if trade were to flourish without chronic payments difficulties, European discrimination against the Dollar Area would have to be permanent.

In the light not only of more recent events, but also of developments that had been gathering momentum since about 1950, it is surely remarkable that such a statement could have been made by a distinguished economist in 1957.[4] In fairness to Crowther, it should be recalled that his lecture was delivered during the Suez crisis when, for a time, European dollar difficulties threatened to reappear. Be that as it may, 1957 is the last year that a plausible financial case for permanent European commercial discrimination against the United States could have been made. To understand what has happened, it will be helpful, first, to review briefly certain trends in the American balance of payments since the war; second, to note what has happened to European monetary reserves; and, third, to examine the implications of the return to convertibility of the leading European currencies.

[3] *Balances and Imbalances of Payments* (Boston: Graduate School of Business Administration, Harvard University, 1957), p. 48. The same theme is developed in Crowther's Weinstock lecture at the University of California. This appeared as a booklet entitled *The Morality of Discrimination in International Trade* (Berkeley: University of California, 1957).

[4] Equally recent, but more balanced and comprehensive, is Sir Donald MacDougall's *The World Dollar Problem: A Study in International Economics* (London: Macmillan, 1957).

Reversal in the United States Balance of Payments

Surely the most striking feature of the American balance of payments since World War II is the impressive contrast between the pattern before 1949 and the pattern since. In the early postwar years, the international accounts of this country were characterized by a massive over-all "cash" surplus. In other words, the flow of payments from the United States to foreign countries for goods, services, long-term investments, and foreign financial assistance was much less than the corresponding flow of payments from foreign countries to the United States. As a result, foreign countries had to dip deeply into their holdings of gold and dollars to make up the difference. For the three years 1946-48 their net payments of gold and dollars to the United States amounted to $6.7 billion; of this, $3.5 billion, or 52 per cent, came from Western Europe (OEEC countries).

As a result of this grave disequilibrium, the gold reserves of the United States reached an all-time peak of $24.8 billion at the end of August 1949, an amount equal to about 70 per cent of the world's monetary gold at that time. Figures for the same date are not available for Western Europe but, a month later, the combined gold reserves of OEEC countries amounted to only $5.2 billion. In addition, OEEC countries had dollar holdings[5] of $2.2 billion; thus their combined holdings of gold and dollars were only $7.4 billion, whereas the external short-term liabilities of the United Kingdom alone amounted in mid-1949 to $15.0 billion.[6]

Since 1949 this situation has radically changed. In striking

[5] The term "dollar holdings" here refers to both official and private dollar balances, whether in the form of demand or time deposits or in the form of holdings of United States government securities.

[6] At the old rate of exchange. By the end of 1949, external liabilities were somewhat higher in terms of sterling but, because of devaluation, their equivalent in dollars had dropped to $11.0 billion.

contrast to the early postwar years, the United States, for considerably more than a decade, has been in over-all deficit with foreign countries. That is to say, the United States has experienced a net loss of gold and dollars to foreign countries in every calendar year since 1949.[7] For the fourteen-year period 1950-63 this cash deficit aggregated $27.0 billion, of which $9.8 billion was settled in gold and $17.2 billion, or 64 per cent, in dollars (i.e., in an increase in the dollar liabilities owed to foreign countries). Actually, the data show a slight deficit for the year 1949 itself, but the figure is so small that 1949 may best be regarded as a year of balance separating a period of heavy over-all surplus from the subsequent years of persistent deficit.[8]

Significantly, the lion's share of the American deficit has been with Western Europe. For the period 1950-63 Western Europe accounted for 68 per cent of the cash deficit with foreign countries.

Though this is not the place to enter into a long discussion of the causes of the shift in the American balance of payments, it will be useful to indicate a few important developments. If we compare an early postwar year, say 1947, with a recent year, such as 1963, the fact which emerges most forcefully is that while exports of goods and services (excluding income from private foreign investments, which we shall consider separately) have increased by 46 per cent, imports of goods and services (even if we exclude military expenditures, which are treated as an import item in the official figures) have exactly tripled. In absolute terms, the export surplus of goods and services, excluding private invest-

[7] These figures exclude the American balance of payments with international institutions. If such transactions are included, the United States had a small cash surplus in 1957.

[8] While 1949 was a year of balance, it was by no means a year of equilibrium, since the balance would not have occurred in the absence of massive American financial assistance combined with exceedingly tight foreign restrictions on American exports.

ment income and American military expenditures abroad, fell from $10.9 billion in 1947 to $3.9 billion in 1963.

Much has been made in recent years of the expanding net out-flow of private long-term capital, which in 1963 amounted to $3.5 billion, compared with a figure of $798 million in 1947. What is often overlooked, however, is that the net outflow of private in-vestment funds has been more than offset by the expanding inflow of income from American investments abroad. Thus the net out-flow of private long-term capital was $2.7 billion higher in 1963 than in 1947, but the return flow of income from private foreign investment was $3.4 billion higher. Over the postwar period as a whole, these two related developments have on balance been a source of strength rather than of strain in the American balance of payments.

Similarly, the outflow of "extraordinary expenditures" (gov-ernment grants, net government loans, plus military expenditures abroad) does nothing to explain the *reversal* in the American balance of payments which took place after 1949. While the com-position of such expenditures has greatly changed, the annual total generally has fluctuated within moderate limits and, indeed, was slightly less in 1962 ($6.4 billion) than in 1947 ($6.6 billion).[9] In accounting for the shift from a $4.6 billion cash surplus in 1947 to a cash deficit of over $2 billion in 1963, this flow of payments is clearly of no help whatever.

It is true, of course, that extraordinary expenditures have in recent years substantially exceeded the export surplus of goods and services, but the basic reason for the change from an over-all surplus to an over-all deficit in the American balance-of-pay-

---

[9] These figures include American transactions with international institu-tions, but the figure for 1947 does not include the United States capital con-tribution of $2,745 million to the International Monetary Fund. If the latter figure were included, the contrast between the total of extraordinary expendi-tures in 1947 and the total in 1962 would, of course, be much greater.

ments has been the sharp decline in the export surplus. This decline has been attributable, as we have seen, to the fact that exports (including services) have expanded much more slowly than imports. The drop in the export surplus has been particularly abrupt in relation to Western Europe. While American exports of goods and services to Western Europe (excluding private investment income) were only about two-fifths higher in 1963 than in 1947, imports of goods and services from that area (excluding military expenditures) were almost exactly five times as high. As a result, the export surplus (thus defined) with Western Europe was $3.4 billion lower in 1963 than in 1947.

While the growth in American imports, particularly from Western Europe, has been rapid, there is really nothing surprising about this development. It has long been observed that a country's imports, including its imports of services, tend to vary with its level of economic activity, as measured by such indictators as industrial production or gross national product. For the United States, the relationship between imports and total output tends to vary little from year to year. Thus, expressed as a percentage of gross national product, American imports of goods and services (excluding military expenditures) were only moderately higher in 1963 (4.0 per cent) than in 1947 (3.3 per cent). And if imports from Western Europe are excluded, the ratio of imports to gross national product is the same in both years, the figure in each case being 2.6 per cent.

Nor is the particularly sharp increase in American imports from Western Europe difficult to explain. A development of this kind was the readily predictable result of the reconstruction, with American help, of European productive capacity. Inevitably that recovery manifested itself in increased competition with the United States in terms of price, quality, and delivery dates. Also contributing to the increase in Western European sales to the American market were a large number of exchange-rate adjustments, notably the devaluations of September 1949. In this connection it is significant that 1949, as previously stated, separated a period of an American balance-of-payments surplus from the following period of over-all deficit.

Disappearance of the "Concealed" Dollar Problem

The situation since 1949 is in such dramatic contrast to the situation in the early postwar years that the reader may wonder why it did not receive more prompt attention. Actually there is no great mystery about this. In the first place, the American cash deficit with foreign countries did not reach alarming proportions until 1958, when it abruptly attained a level of $3.4 billion ($3.0 billion of which was with Western Europe). In the second place, the deficit led to an increase in foreign monetary reserves, and this was properly regarded as a welcome development by the American government at a time when foreign reserves were gravely inadequate.

Finally, the transition from a position of surplus to one of deficit did not in itself signal an end to the world dollar problem. As was frequently pointed out at the time, there remained in the early 1950's a "dollar gap" concealed, on the one hand, by large American extraordinary expenditures abroad and, on the other, by exceedingly tight foreign quantitative restrictions on purchases from the Dollar Area. Thus, as we have seen, it was possible as late as 1957 to make a more or less plausible case for the proposition that the world dollar problem not only was still with us but would be with us indefinitely. It is therefore necessary to comment briefly on extraordinary expenditures and on quantitative restrictions.

First, let us consider extraordinary expenditures which, as already noted, have remained at a high and fairly stable annual level. If the analysis is to get below the surface, it is necessary to distinguish sharply between expenditures which were motivated by foreign balance-of-payments difficulties and expenditures which were motivated by other considerations. In the early postwar years (say through mid-1950) American extraordinary expenditures abroad were primarily in response to a situation of acute international disequilibrium mainly involving Western Europe, on the one side, and the United States, on the other. The main counterpart of these expenditures was the massive Western European trade deficit with the United States that prevailed during these years. To a major extent this deficit was a planned deficit, reflecting a remarkable joint undertaking in economic reconstruction.

Since 1950, however, and particularly since 1952, American extraordinary expenditures abroad have not been mainly motivated by considerations of international disequilibrium. Following the outbreak of the Korean war in mid-1950, the major purpose of such spending quickly shifted from economic reconstruction to mutual defense. After 1952 much the most important form of extraordinary expenditure was not government grants or loans but American military expenditures abroad, a comprehensive classification including such items as the spending of American troops stationed in foreign countries, purchases abroad by the U.S. military authorities, and American defense construction abroad. While extraordinary in the sense of being of governmental rather than of private origin, such expenditures have been dictated not by balance-of-payments considerations, but by the dangerous international political situation. The point of this is that, while it made sense in the early postwar years to refer to a dollar gap concealed by American extraordinary expenditures abroad, it has made little sense during the past decade, since such expenditures, particularly in the case of Western Europe, have lost their original character as foreign aid and have become instead the American contribution to a common defense effort.

This conclusion does not, of course, dispose of the dollar gap which for a long period was concealed by foreign quantitative restrictions. As late as January 1953, only 11 per cent of Western European (OEEC) imports from the United States and Canada were not restricted by quotas. Under such conditions, it was not possible (despite the reversal in the American balance of payments) to make a convincing case for the disappearance of the dollar problem since it could always be argued that, in the absence of these abnormal restrictions, American exports would greatly increase, and the balance of payments would revert to a position of surplus.

From 1953 on, however, European quantitative restrictions on American exports began to decline sharply, and by the end of 1958 about three-fourths of Western European imports from the Dollar Area were quota-free. Indeed, several European countries had removed almost all quotas on such imports and no longer treated them less favorably than imports from OEEC countries.

As was widely expected, the return to convertibility of the major European currencies at the end of 1958 stimulated the removal of most of the remaining quotas on dollar goods (excluding foodstuffs). While such restrictions still exist in a few countries and for a few products, their purpose has shifted from protecting the balance of payments to protecting certain industries from outside competition. Accordingly, just as it is no longer possible to speak of a European dollar gap concealed by extraordinary expenditures, so is it no longer possible to speak of a European dollar gap concealed by European import quotas.

Implications of the Return to Convertibility

The shift in the American balance of payments has been the principal factor responsible for two developments which, taken together, have removed any purely financial justification for a regional approach to the removal of Western European trade barriers. The first of these developments is the rapid increase in

Western European monetary reserves, particularly after 1952. From the end of 1949 to the end of 1963 Western European holdings of gold and dollars increased by approximately four times, rising from $8.3 billion to $31.2 billion. Between the same dates the share of Western European holdings in the total of gold and dollars held by foreign countries increased from slightly over half to about two-thirds. For the Six the rise in reserves has been particularly spectacular. Gold and dollar holdings of the Six at the end of 1963 were over six times as high as at the end of 1949, having risen from $2.8 billion to $18.4 billion. During the same period American gold reserves fell from almost $25 billion to well under $16 billion. The result of this rather drastic redistribution of monetary reserves among the Atlantic partners has been to restore Western Europe to a strong international financial position, while still leaving the United States with 37 per cent of the free world's monetary gold.

The second development is the return to convertibility of sterling and the other major European currencies. Until the late 1950s, currency inconvertibility was frequently cited as the justification for Western European discrimination in the application of trade barriers. In an article on trade policy published in 1956, a former United States Treasury official wrote that "The tendency to consider trade discrimination inevitable until currency convertibility has been achieved . . . has been the most discouraging feature of postwar economic policy."[10]

Whether discouraging or not, such a tendency has not been difficult to understand. It was most in evidence, of course, in the years immediately after the war. In the days before the European Payments Union, when European trade was governed by bilateral agreements, a Belgian payments surplus with France, for example, could not be used to finance a payments deficit with Sweden be-

[10] George Bronz, "An International Trade Organization: The Second Attempt," *Harvard Law Review*, January 1956, p. 459.

cause the French franc was inconvertible not only into dollars but into Swedish kroner. Under such a regime countries naturally strove to achieve a high degree of bilateral balance and could usually do so only by highly discriminatory trade policies.

As was shown in Chapter 2, the creation of the European Payments Union in 1950 completely removed the financial incentive for trade discrimination *within* the OEEC area by making OEEC currencies convertible into one another. But Western European currencies remained inconvertible into dollars, and the rapid removal of intra-European quantitative restrictions during the first two years of the Union was unaccompanied by any serious effort to tackle the restrictions in effect against goods from the Dollar Area.

As early as 1953, foreign-exchange markets along traditional lines were re-established in Western European financial centers, but the dollar could not be bought or sold in these markets. Since 1958, however, the major Western European currencies have returned to convertibility with the dollar. The result has been that dollars, sterling, lire, deutsche marks, and guilders are interchangeable and are therefore of equivalent attractiveness or "hardness." In these circumstances there is no longer any financial incentive for a European country to treat transactions with the United States less favorably than those with the United Kingdom, Italy, Germany, or the other countries that have moved to convertibility. Consequently, the financial justification for an intra-European approach to the removal of trade restrictions has entirely disappeared.

The Economic Case for a Regional Approach in Western Europe

The disappearance of dollar shortage, of inadequate reserves and inconvertibility in Western Europe does not, of course, dispose of the entire economic basis for a regional approach to European problems. Much of the interest in a common market rests on entirely different economic considerations—in particular, on the conviction that Western Europe as a group of individually protected national units is economically inefficient and outmoded.

For several decades this point of view has appealed to a growing number of thoughtful Europeans, who derive much of their inspiration from the United States as a large free-trade area. The view is well expressed in the words of Count Coudenhove-Kalergi, the celebrated exponent of European unification during the interwar period, who wrote that "in the creation of a large European market without internal tariff protection lay the only hope of a quick rise in the European standard of living. The forty-eight American states offered to the world the unaccustomed spectacle of mass-prosperity, based on the interplay of mass-production and mass-consumption, high wages and relatively low prices. Clearly, such prosperity would have been unthinkable if each of the forty-eight states had been economically surrounded by a barrier."[11]

This train of thought, which is also prominent in the writings of Jean Monnet, the great implementer of the Count's dream, has a strong intuitive appeal and has provided much of the drive behind the move toward a United States of Europe. It rests on several distinct considerations: on the increased efficiency resulting from the new opportunities for specialization; on the beneficial effects on price and quality of the increased international competition; on the lower costs of production attainable through "economies of scale"; on the higher rate of investment, fed partly from outside sources, induced by the increased opportunities for profit in a wider market; and on the improved quality of plant and equipment resulting from the accelerated retooling of industry

[11] Count Coudenhove-Kalergi, *An Idea Conquers the World* (New York: Roy Publishers, 1954), pp. 82-83.

66

with capital goods reflecting the latest technological developments.

The removal of trade barriers within Western Europe may be thought of as an extension of the earlier efforts to remove such barriers within the present Western European national units. The achievement of free trade within national boundaries has in some cases been a relatively recent development, and has followed no particular pattern. In France, for example, national unification preceded the attainment of internal free trade. Prior to the French Revolution customhouses operated at many provincial border points within France, and the efforts of Turgot in 1774 to end this regime met with strong opposition. Not until after the Revolution was internal free trade firmly established.

In Germany the removal of trade barriers between the many petty states preceded political unification. The process of achieving free trade within what was later to become modern Germany took several decades. As late as 1800 Prussia alone had over sixty different tariff regimes. In 1818 a uniform tariff was established for the whole kingdom, and other German states were invited to join Prussia in a customs union. By 1834 seventeen German states had become members of the *Zollverein*, and by 1867 the union included all the German territory (except the Free Cities of Hamburg and Bremen) that was shortly to become Imperial Germany.[12]

There can be little doubt that the attainment of free trade within the several national states contributed immensely to the economic development of Western Europe. By the same token, it would seem likely that the removal of national trade barriers within Western

[12] See also Jacob Viner, *The Customs Union Issue* (New York: Carnegie Endowment for International Peace, 1950), Chapter V. Viner points out that for several European countries, including Denmark, Switzerland, and the United Kingdom (with respect to Ireland), internal free trade was not fully achieved until well into the nineteenth century, and that for one country (Russia under the Czars) it was never achieved.

Europe would confer great additional economic benefits. Indeed, what the leaders of European union in effect are saying is that tariff-enclosed national units the size of Italy or France are just as much of an anachronism in the mid-twentieth century as were tariff-enclosed provinces in the mid-eighteenth. Viewed in such a light, the trend toward regional economic union is the natural result of developments in transportation, communication, and industrial technology in a jet age.

This intuition may be correct, but it would be a mistake to regard the case for regional free trade as self-evident. Actually, the case is neither simple nor watertight. As Professor Viner has ably shown, the removal of tariffs within a group of countries, when unaccompanied by the removal of tariffs against the outside world, is not an unmixed blessing. Trade and production may be directed into uneconomic as well as into economic channels, and in extreme cases the net economic effects conceivably may be unfavorable. Viner makes no such gloomy predictions with respect to Western Europe; on the contrary, he explicitly concludes that a Western European customs union would in all likelihood be economically beneficial.[13] But the question he raises is of importance to any evaluation of European economic integration that hopes to get below the surface, and it will be useful to examine briefly his line of reasoning.

Let us, then, imagine a situation in which a small number of countries (say a hypothetical "Six") decide to remove their trade barriers among themselves while leaving intact their barriers

[13] His exact language is as follows: "On economic grounds, there can be little basis for reasonable doubt that the formation of a customs union embracing all or most of Western Europe, or even smaller customs unions which included at least several important countries with substantial overlapping in their ranges of heavily protected industries, would, in the net, contribute both to the economic recovery of Western Europe, once the necessary adjustments had ben made, and to a greater degree of international specialization of production." Viner, cited, p. 133.

against the outside world. For the sake of simplicity, we shall assume that tariffs are the only obstacle to trade and, to avoid some tiresome exposition, that tariff schedules are uniform for each of the six countries. The latter supposition will permit us to assume that, after intraregional tariffs are removed, the region will automatically have a common tariff wall with the outside world without the necessity for any member country to raise or to lower its duties. The assumption will also make it unnecessary to be concerned about whether the arrangement is a customs union or a free-trade area since, in this situation, the tariff changes would be the same in either case (*i.e.*, would be strictly intraregional).

Under these assumptions, as Professor Viner has shown, the removal of tariffs within the region will tend to have two effects on trade: a "trade-creating" effect, which is good; and a "trade-diverting" effect, which is bad. The first effect occurs when, as a result of the removal of intraregional tariffs, a member country (say, Italy) imports a commodity which, because of the tariff, it had previously produced itself. In this situation consumers in Italy obtain the commodity from a cheaper source than under the old regime. Trade of this type is therefore economic and, as Viner points out, is a step in the right direction even if the commodity might, under completely free trade, be obtained still more cheaply from a source outside the region.

The same cannot be said, however, of trade diversion. Trade diversion occurs when, as a result of the removal of intraregional tariffs, a member country (say, Italy) now imports from another member country (say, France) a commodity that it formerly imported from a source outside the region (say, the United States). Such a result will take place when the price of the now duty-free item from France is lower than the American price plus duty. For example, suppose that before duty the price of the item is $10 when purchased from France and $8 when purchased from the

United States. Suppose also that before the formation of the customs union the Italian duty on the item is 50 per cent. Under these conditions, Italian consumers buy the commodity from the United States, where the price plus duty is $12 per unit, instead of from France, where the price plus duty is $15. After the removal of intraregional tariffs, however, the price of the French product in Italy falls to $10, while the American price remains at $12. Consequently, Italians now buy the item from France rather than from the United States. Thus trade has been diverted rather than created.

But why is this situation uneconomic? Isn't the Italian consumer better off because he now gets the commodity for $10 per unit, whereas before the removal of intraregional tariffs he paid $12? The answer is that in this type of situation the saving to the consumer is always outweighed by the loss of customs revenue to the government. In the case we have just considered the saving to the consumer is $2 per unit, while the loss to the government is $4 (the duty received when imports were from the United States). The net loss to the Italian economy is therefore $2 per unit. Thus if 1 million units per year had formerly been imported from the United States, Italian consumers would save $2 million per year by buying, duty-free, the same amount from France, but the Italian treasury would lose $4 million in annual revenue. With given budgetary objectives, the Italian government presumably would seek to restore this revenue from other sources. If, for example, it were to do so by raising income taxes, Italian consumers would clearly suffer in terms of real income, since a saving of $2 million in the import bill would be more than offset by a reduction of $4 million in disposable income. Alternatively, the Italian government, instead of recouping the loss in customs revenue, might reduce governmental services by $4 million. In this case, a saving of $2 million on imports would be outweighed by a $4 million reduction in public services. The point is that, however the effects are manifested in any particular case, trade diversion involves a net economic burden to a country because imports are obtained from a higher cost source.

Since the removal of tariffs on a regional basis tends to have both trade-creating and trade-diverting effects, it is not possible to state categorically whether, on balance, a move to intraregional free trade will be economically beneficial or detrimental. Nevertheless, if certain facts about the region are known, it is possible to make a number of dependable generalizations. Speaking broadly, one can say that intraregional free trade is more likely to be predominantly trade-creating (1) the larger the region, (2) the greater the degree of national protection provided by tariffs before their removal within the region, (3) the greater the national differences within the region in the cost of producing the same product, and (4) the lower the level of tariffs with the outside world.[14] Let us consider briefly each of these generalizations.

First, it is evident that the larger a customs union or free-trade area, the more likely it is that trade creation will exceed trade diversion. Clearly, the internal economic effects of a customs union consisting of the whole world except New Guinea would differ little from those of a world characterized by completely free trade. On this basis, Benelux is a more questionable economic arrangement (from an internal point of view) than a customs union of the Six, and a customs union of the Six is a less desirable arrangement than a union embracing all of Western Europe.

Second, it should be clear that opportunities for trade creation are greatest when national self-sufficiency, because of trade barriers, has been at a high level. Trade creation occurs when imports are substituted for protected higher-cost domestic production, and it is economically beneficial for precisely that reason.

Third, the regional potentialities for trade creation, as well as

[14] For a longer list of conditions, see Viner, cited, pp. 51-52.

the degree of benefit conferred by trade creation, depend on the degree to which the cost of producing the same commodity differs from country to country within the region. Production costs will vary with national differences in natural resources, labor skills, capital equipment, distance from markets, and many other factors. In a region as heterogeneous as Western Europe, the presumption is strong that wide differences in national production costs will be numerous.

Finally, it is obvious that the potentialities for trade diversion in a customs union or free-trade area will diminish with a fall in the level of external tariffs, and will disappear completely if external tariffs are entirely eliminated.

Trade Creation, Trade Diversion, and the Common Market

In terms of these four criteria, the European Economic Community would appear to stand up rather well. In the first place, the region is large and may eventually become larger. In the second place, it includes countries, such as Italy and France, which in the past have maintained highly protected national markets— markets, moreover, in which the protection appears in substantial measure to have been directed against countries which are now partners in the Community. In the third place, a region which embraces countries as diverse in resources and skills as France and the Netherland, or as Italy and Germany, is likely to have numerous wide differences in national production costs.

On the fourth criterion, the height of the common external tariff, we shall have much to say later. One point which deserves special emphasis, however, is that tariff discrimination within Western Europe is being introduced, not into a historical situation of nondiscrimination, but rather into a situation in which, until recent years, there was a high degree of Western European trade discrimination against the outside world. This discrimination was implemented not by tariffs, but by exceedingly stringent quantitative restrictions. Since 1952, as we have seen, European discrimination against outside countries has steadily declined, and this decline has accelerated since the return to convertibility of most Western European currencies at the end of 1958.

The reduction in Western European discrimination complicates the analysis of such developments as the European Economic Community and the European Free Trade Association. For the increase in tariff discrimination which these institutions have set in motion must be examined against a background of greatly reduced discrimination in a form of trade barrier which, during most of the past three decades, has been a much more serious obstacle to international trade than tariffs. It is clearly the net effect of these two opposing trends that is significant, and there is hardly room for doubt that during the first three or four years of the Community's existence the net effect of all changes in trade restrictions was a reduction, rather than an increase, in Western European commercial discrimination against the outside world.

This situation, however, cannot be expected to continue. Except under the most optimistic assumptions, some trade diversion is likely to occur. In terms of commodities, the danger is greatest in foodstuffs, which, on the average, are likely to encounter a considerable increase in the level of protection. In terms of countries, the danger is greatest in the low-tariff members of the Community, namely, Germany and the Benelux group. In these countries quantitative restrictions (outside agriculture) have been almost entirely removed from intra-European trade, and for several years there has been virtually no discrimination in this sphere against the outside world. Thus, what happens in the field of tariffs is very important. We have seen that participation in a customs union may lead to trade diversion even if external tariffs are not raised at all; but the Benelux countries and Germany, as low-tariff members of the Community, will be required to raise many external tariffs substantially. In such circumstances, some trade diversion is almost bound to occur.

On the other hand, for the high-tariff members of the Community, France and Italy, the introduction of regional free trade may be predominantly trade creating. These countries will not only be removing tariffs within the Community, they will also be sharply reducing tariffs with the rest of the world. Moreover, Italy and France are countries which until recent years have been highly discriminatory in the application of quantitative restrictions, and the removal of discrimination in this sphere may largely offset the introduction of tariff discrimination.

Much depends, of course, on the height of the Community's common external tariff and, in particular, on the height of the common barriers against imports of foodstuffs. One point is clear: it is strongly in the economic interest both of the Community and of the United States that these restrictions be at the lowest attainable level.

5

The Changing Pattern of Atlantic Tariffs

Theory is always simpler than reality. Even when it seems terribly complex, it is still "simpliste," as compared to the range of factors operating as conditions, as means, or as ends, in any actual concrete situation.

JACOB VINER, 1952

It is now time to move from the realm of theory to the "actual concrete situation," to use Professor Viner's words. The preceding chapter set forth the economic case for European integration—or, more precisely, for the regional removal of trade barriers—but the analysis remained on a somewhat general and theoretical plane since no information was provided about the level of Western European tariffs. In order to pass judgment on such matters as whether "trade diversion" is likely to be important or unimportant in the Six and the Seven, it clearly is necessary to know something about the recent and prospective degrees of protection in those areas; and in order to determine the implications for American policy of the rapidly changing pattern of European tariffs, it is also necessary to know something about the structure of tariffs in the United States. Accordingly, the present chapter is devoted to the important subject of Atlantic tariffs.

Inevitably, such a factual survey will be in the nature of a bird's-eye view. A thoroughly adequate account of Atlantic tariff levels and of the probable effects of prospective tariff changes would require an enormous amount of detailed commodity information and analysis which could easily fill a scholarly work of several volumes. Our aim must perforce be far more modest. We shall endeavor in this chapter to derive a few broad but significant conclusions, chiefly of a statistical nature, which will enable us to form a better judgment of the economic importance of the tariff developments associated with the Six and the Seven and provide perspective for our later review of American policy.

Fortunately, much of the arduous spadework has already been done by others. Two outstanding recent studies, one British and the other American, have compiled on a comparable basis a vast amount of detailed tariff information for the Atlantic countries. The first study, *Atlantic Tariffs and Trade*,[1] provides comparative tariff rates for the European Economic Community, the European Free Trade Association, Canada, and the United States. In greater detail, the second study, *Comparative Tariffs and Trade: The United States and the European Common Market*,[2] compares the American tariff with the prospective common external tariff of the Community. These admirable studies have immensely simplified the problem of making significant tariff comparisons and provide the foundation for what hopefully will be a wealth of penetrating future research.

Some Difficulties

Before proceeding further it will be useful to introduce two important caveats. These are offered not as counsels of despair or of complete skepticism in tariff matters, but as words of caution. The first warning is that the height of a tariff is usually, but not necessarily, a good indication of its protective strength. In certain

[1] Prepared by the British research organization, PEP (Political and Economic Planning); London: Allen & Unwin, 1962.
[2] Prepared by Frances K. Topping; New York: Committee for Economic Development, 1963. In two volumes.

cases an apparently high duty, because it has little effect on the volume of imports, may properly be regarded as a revenue duty rather than as a protective duty. In other cases a duty which appears to be low may actually be prohibitive—that is, may be high enough virtually to exclude imports of the product on which it is levied. The protectiveness of a duty, in other words, depends not only on its height but also on such factors as the pattern of demand and supply for the product and the relation of domestic to foreign costs of production. Thus, in one case, a modest reduction in duty may be of great significance while, in another case, a major reduction may accomplish little because the reduced duty is still highly protective.

The second warning is that the measurement of tariff levels is notoriously full of troublesome difficulties. A measure frequently employed—the ratio of customs receipts to the value of imports —is particularly unreliable, since duties which are genuinely prohibitive bring in no revenue. Thus, as Professor Viner has pointed out, if a country were to apply a very high duty to the goods it wished to keep out, while letting all other goods come in duty-free, customs receipts would be zero, and the resulting ratio of customs receipts to the value of imports would be the same as for a country with completely free trade. By this standard, such a country, which might have by far the highest tariffs in the world, would appear to have a greater degree of freedom of trade than a country which imposed a revenue duty of two per cent on all imports.

The same observation can be made about averages of tariff rates in which each rate is weighted according to the relative importance of the commodity in total imports.[3] Averages of this

[3] Indeed, a little arithmetic will show that the ratio of customs receipts to the value of imports is exactly the same figure as an average of tariff rates weighted according to the relative share of each product in total imports. Thus, tariff investigators who wish the latter figure can save themselves an immense amount of work simply by making the former calculation.

kind, while widely used, invariably have a downward bias, since protective duties—to the extent that they are protective—restrict imports of the protected products and thereby reduce their weights in the average. Indeed, prohibitive duties (duties which completely bar imports) do not appear in the average at all, since the affected commodities are assigned a weight of zero.

Because of these difficulties, unweighted averages of tariff rates are sometimes employed as a measure of tariff levels. These have the advantage of being free from a downward bias since each duty, in effect, is assigned an equal weight. Whatever else may be said about them, such averages may be regarded as a good reflection of the tariff mentality prevailing in a particular country, especially in those sectors (notably the broad sector of manufactured goods) where tariffs are almost universally applied. Precisely because they treat all duties alike, unweighted averages may be regarded as a good measure of the level of rates that tariff-makers are in the habit of legislating or decreeing.

This does not mean that an unweighted average is an ideal measure of tariff levels. Presumably the best measure would be an average weighted according to the commodity composition of imports under a regime of completely free trade. In the absence of controlled experiments with free trade, however, it is notoriously difficult, if not impossible, to obtain reliable estimates of what such weights should be, particularly in the high-tariff countries.

In view of these problems, probably the best procedure is simply to compare the various types of available tariff averages and to supplement this information with other data—in particular, with measures of the range and frequency of tariff rates. From such information it is possible to draw a number of significant conclusions. If, for example, the unweighted average of tariff rates in a given case is considerably higher than the weighted average, two conclusions can be deduced. The first is that the country being examined has a wide range of tariff rates, and the second is that the higher rates provide a considerable measure of protection—that is, have a strong tendency (as of course intended) to restrict imports. It should be noted, however, that the converse of these propositions is not necessarily true. In situations where the weighted average of customs duties is approximately the same as the unweighted average, it is *not* possible to conclude that the duties provide little protection; the more probable explanation is that most or all of the duties fall within a narrow range. Fortunately, the range and frequency of tariffs in the Atlantic countries are matters which, because of the recent PEP and CED tariff studies, can now be easily determined.

Over-all Tariff Averages in the Atlantic Countries

With these words of caution in mind, let us first take a quick look at tariff averages which cover all imports, including those for which the duty is zero. Such averages are only of limited interest, since tariffs typically vary widely in height from one commodity group to another and in one important category, foodstuffs, are commonly accompanied by other forms of import restriction. Nevertheless, some useful impressions may be gained, particularly from a comparison of weighted with unweighted averages.

Unweighted over-all tariff averages are available from several sources. In 1952 a GATT study covering a considerable number of countries provided over-all unweighted averages of tariff rates for the 570 import items in the Standard International Trade Classification.[4] A Swiss study, published in 1959, presented unweighted tariff averages for the Common Market countries and Switzerland which reflect the tariff situation prevailing shortly

[4] *International Trade, 1952* (Geneva: GATT, 1953), p. 62.

before the Rome Treaty went into effect.[5] In 1964 a memorandum prepared by the staff of the European Economic Community provided unweighted averages for the EEC common external tariff, the United Kingdom tariff, and the United States tariff.[6]

These averages are shown in Table 1. Except where important tariff changes have taken place, the figures in the three studies agree closely. Thus, the discrepancy in the average for Italy is largely explained by an administrative reduction in the Italian tariff, while the low EEC figure for the Community's common tariff takes into account the duty reductions in the 1961 GATT Agreement.[7]

Table 1 also compares the results of the foregoing studies with two weighted measures of over-all tariff levels. The first of these measures, where available, is the ratio of customs receipts to total value of imports (in most cases, for the year 1961). The second is an average of tariff rates, computed by the Committee for Economic Development, for the United States and for the European Economic Community, with each rate weighted according to the share of the corresponding commodity in total imports.[8]

[5] Hans Christoph Binswanger, "Der Zollschutz in den Ländern der Europäischen Wirtschaftsgemeinschaft und in der Schweiz," in *Die europäische Wirtschaftsintegration im Banne des Gemeinsamen Marktes*, Schweizerischen Institut für Aussenwirtschafts- und Marktforschung an der Handels-Hochschule St. Gallen (Zurich and St. Gallen: Polygraphischer Verlag AG, 1959), pp. 119-152. (This book is also Nos. 1 and 2 of 1959 of the journal, *Aussenwirtschaft*.) The figures on the Common Market were taken from Raymond Bertrand, *Comparaison du niveau des tarifs douaniers des pays du marché commun* (Paris: Institut de Science Economique Appliquée, 1958); they covered 1,910 items in the Brussels tariff classification. The figure for Switzerland covered 1,650 items in the Swiss tariff.

[6] The EEC averages exclude agricultural products. European Economic Community, *Information Memo P/64*, Brussels, 1964.

[7] The EEC figures for the United Kingdom and the United States do not take into account the 1961 GATT ("Dillon round") duty reductions; the study concludes that these would not reduce the British and American tariff averages by more than one percentage point.

[8] The CED averages exclude foodstuffs and beverages and do not take into account the tariff cuts made under the 1961 GATT Agreement.

TABLE 1

Average Tariff Rates for All Imports in the Six, the Seven, and the United States
(In per cent)

	Unweighted Averages			Weighted Measures	
	GATT Tariff Averages for 1952	Swiss Study Figures for 1955	EEC Study Figures[a]	Customs Revenue as % of Imports in 1961	CED Study Figures[b]
EEC Countries					
Benelux	9	9.5		5.4	
France	19	18.1		5.2[c]	
Germany	16	15.5[d]			
Italy	24	17.3			
EEC Common Tariff	17[e]	15.1[e]	11.7[f]		5.2[g]
EFTA Countries					
Austria	17			8.5	
Denmark	5				
Norway				3.6	
Portugal				14.2[c]	
Sweden	6			5.3	
Switzerland		10.2		9.0	
United Kingdom	17		18.4		
United States	16		17.8	7.3	7.8[h]

[a] Averages exclude agricultural products.
[b] Averages exclude foodstuffs and beverages and do not take into account duty reductions under the 1961 GATT Agreement.
[c] Figure for 1959.
[d] German tariffs were reduced by about 20 per cent in 1959, but this reduction was not permitted to affect the level of the EEC common tariff which, with certain exceptions, is based on the duties in effect on January 1, 1957.
[e] Unweighted average for four customs areas.
[f] Adjusted for duty reductions under the 1961 GATT Agreement.
[g] Weighted by 1959 net imports.
[h] Weighted by 1960 imports.
Source: See text.

The most conspicuous fact about the table is the sharp disparity between the weighted and the unweighted measures of tariff levels. Indeed, from the weighted measures one might easily gain the impression that, with the possible exception of Portugal, the North Atlantic countries could reasonably be described as low-tariff countries. That such an impression is misleading is revealed by the unweighted measures which, in all cases where a comparison can be made, are higher—and usually are much higher—than the weighted measures. The disparity is, of course, exactly what would be expected where tariffs reveal a considerable range and where the higher duties have a strong tendency to restrict imports. Accordingly, it is difficult to escape the conclusion that in those cases where the disparity is large the weighted measures seriously understate the actual tariff levels.

Tariff Levels by Commodity Groups

Even at best, however, over-all averages reveal only a little about tariff behavior. Tariff levels typically vary widely from one commodity group to another, and for purposes of analysis it will greatly simplify matters if we divide imported products into three broad categories: foodstuffs, industrial raw materials, and manufactured goods.

In the case of foodstuffs a high degree of protection is the rule both in Western Europe and in the United States. In this sector, however, protection is frequently effected by devices other than tariffs. Import quotas and export subsidies are widely used, and under its common agricultural policy, the European Economic Community plans to rely heavily on "variable import levies." Under such conditions customs duties, although widely applied to agricultural products, are frequently of secondary importance in relation to other methods of protection. Consequently, in this category, averages of tariff rates—whether weighted or unweighted—are particularly unreliable as measures of the degree of protection actually in effect.[9]

In the case of industrial raw materials the story is very different. With certain exceptions, this sector is characterized by a high degree of freedom both from tariffs and from other forms of protection. There are at least two reasons for this situation. In the first place, many of such commodities are not produced in the North Atlantic countries, and thus there is no incentive to levy tariffs or to impose quotas to protect domestic production.[10] In the second place, even in those cases where domestic production is important, the need for cheap raw materials in order to compete successfully in international trade is so apparent that the political pressures opposed to protection are usually stronger than the pressures favoring protective action. Consequently, while raw materials are occasionally protected by tariffs or quotas, average duties in most industrial countries are low. In Table 2, average duties of 110 "basic materials" are shown for the countries of the European Economic Community and the European Free Trade Association (with the exception of Portugal). The averages are unweighted and include commodities—for most countries, the great majority—on which the duty is zero.

From Table 2 it is evident that most Western European countries pursue a policy of largely free trade in raw materials. Of the countries listed, only Italy has a tariff average higher than 4 per cent, and the prospective EEC common tariff on raw materials is scheduled to average well below 3 per cent.[11] Protective duties in this sector are rare, though a few commodities are protected (no-

[9] An additional difficulty in computing meaningful tariff averages in this sector is that duties on foodstuffs often vary seasonally.

[10] In certain cases, however, there may be an incentive to protect production in dependent, or formerly dependent, overseas countries.

[11] The figure of 2.9 per cent in the table does not take into account the "Dillon round" duty reductions of 1961.

TABLE 2

Average Duties in Western Europe on 110 Basic Materials

(In per cent)

EEC Countries[a]	
Benelux	0.6
France	3.2
Germany	1.2
Italy	6.6
EEC Comon External Tariff	2.9[b]
EFTA Countries[c]	
Austria	2.5
Denmark	0.1
Norway	0.4[d]
Sweden	0.0[e]
Switzerland	2.4
United Kingdom	2.8

[a] The EEC duties here averaged are the "basic rates" used to determine the Community's common external tariff. Except for Italy and in some cases for France, the basic rates are those in effect on January 1, 1957. Italian basic rates are generally about 10 per cent higher than those prevailing in 1957.

[b] Unweighted average for four customs areas.

[c] The EFTA duties here averaged are the legal rates in effect on January 1, 1959.

[d] Excluded from this average are several items which are subject to specific duties for which no *ad valorem* equivalent is available.

[e] All items are duty-free except two, which are subject to specific duties for which no *ad valorem* equivalent is estimated.

Source: PEP, *Tariffs and Trade in Western Europe, A Report* (London: Allen & Unwin, 1959), pp. 2-15.

tably aluminum in the case of France, Italy, and Switzerland; woodpulp in the case of Austria and Italy; and lumber in the case of Italy). In exceptional instances, such as petroleum in the case of France, protection is achieved by quantitative restrictions.

While not included in the table, the United States likewise maintains low or zero duties on most raw materials. In several cases, however, domestic interests have succeeded in obtaining protection. Thus, tungsten and molybdenum are subject to high duties, while imports of lead, zinc, and petroleum are restricted by quotas.

Average Tariffs on Manufactured Goods

In two commodity categories, then, tariffs play a secondary role —in foodstuffs because tariffs are usually supplemented or replaced by other forms of protection, and in raw materials because a high degree of freedom prevails. In the third category, manufactured goods, we find a very different state of affairs. In this sector not only is a substantial degree of tariff protection the rule in most Atlantic countries but, in contrast to the situation a few years ago (when quantitative restrictions were widely applied in Europe to imports of manufactures), tariffs are in most cases the only form of protection employed.

Average tariff rates on manufactured goods for the Six, the Seven, and the United States are presented in Table 3. The first column consists of unweighted averages of tariff levels for 90 groups of manufactured goods, the 90 tariff-level figures themselves being unweighted averages covering large numbers of individual products. This series was prepared by the author from data in Part I of the PEP study, *Atlantic Tariffs and Trade*, which provides the unweighted tariff averages for the 90 commodity groups.[12] The second column presents weighted averages of tariff rates on manufactures for the American tariff and for the prospec-

---

[12] As in the PEP study, manufactured goods are here defined to comprise sections 5 through 8 of the Standard International Trade Classification, excluding groups 682-689 (nonferrous metals). Section 5 covers chemicals; section 6, manufactured goods classified chiefly by material; section 7, machinery and transport equipment; and section 8, miscellaneous manufactured articles. Nonferrous metals are excluded because they are mainly traded in unwrought form, and are therefore here classified as industrial raw materials.

TABLE 3

Average Tariff Rates on Manufactured Goods in the Six, the Seven, and the United States[a]
(In per cent)

	Unweighted Average (PEP)	Weighted Average (CED)
EEC Countries[b]		
Benelux	11.4	
France	17.7	
Germany	8.4	
Italy	19.7	
EEC Common Tariff	14.3[c]	13.0
EFTA Countries		
Austria	17.2	
Denmark	6.7	
Norway	12.0	
Portugal	32.2	
Sweden	8.0	
Switzerland	8.4	
United Kingdom	18.3	
United States	20.2	11.7

[a] Figures do not take into account duty reductions under 1961 GATT Agreement.
[b] See footnote [a], Table 2.
[c] Unweighted average for four customs areas.
Source: See text.

tive common external tariff of the European Economic Community. The figures in this column are derived by the author from data assembled by the Committee for Economic Development. For the United States, tariffs are weighted according to the commodity composition of imports in 1960; for the Community, according to the composition of imports (from countries outside the Community) in 1959. The commodity coverage is virtually the same in both columns.[13]

Several conclusions can be drawn from this table. A comparison with Table 1 reveals that in most Atlantic countries average tariffs for manufactured goods are much higher than for imports as a whole. Since tariff protection is mainly directed at manufactures, this conclusion is, of course, hardly surprising. Moreover, in view of the foregoing analysis, it is hardly surprising that the unweighted averages are higher—and in the American case much higher—than the weighted averages. The disparity is explained in large measure by the restrictive effect on imports (and therefore on the weighting system) of the higher duties. The fact that the disparity is much less for the Community than for the United States must not be construed as evidence that the Community's common tariff will provide little protection; as we shall see shortly, the smaller disparity is rather a reflection of the fact that the Community's duties reveal a much narrower range than those of the United States.

It will be noted that on the basis of the weighted average the Community's common tariff on manufactures is somewhat higher than the American tariff, whereas on the basis of the unweighted average the American tariff on manufactures is much higher than the Community's. On this matter, there can be little doubt that the unweighted average provides the more reliable impression. And that impression is that the United States—like France and

[13] The weighted series is based on a CED memorandum, dated May 3, 1963, summarizing some of the information in the two-volume study, *Comparative Tariffs and Trade: The United States and the European Common Market*, cited. The memorandum contains weighted tariff averages for 75 commodity groups and corresponding import figures. The latter provide the basis for constructing broader weighted averages. For the present purpose, all commodity groups not conforming to the PEP definition of manufactured goods were eliminated.

Italy before the Rome Treaty, and like Portugal and the United Kingdom today—is a high-tariff country.[14]

The figures in Table 3 do not take into account the tariff reductions which are gradually being effected under the 1961 GATT Agreement. The importance of these, however, can easily be overstated. On the American side, most of the tariff reductions appear to have been far below the standard 20 per cent tariff cuts originally envisaged for the "Dillon round."[15] Moreover, these reductions apply to only a modest fraction of the total number of import items. Thus, as already noted, the EEC staff has estimated that the 1961 GATT Agreement would not reduce the over-all American tariff level, or the tariff level of any of the main import subdivisions, by more than one percentage point. In the case of the Community, the impact of the "Dillon round" does not seem to have been much greater. In the EEC "Interim Agreement" with the United States most duty reductions appear to have been in the neighborhood of 20 per cent, but affect only about one-fourth of all manufactured items. Thus, the EEC common tariff on manufactures, as applied to the United States, appears to have been reduced by less than 6 per cent, or from an unweighted average of 14.3 per cent to one of about 13.5 per cent. As in the American case, the reduction was within one percentage point.

[14] It should be pointed out, however, that American *ad valorem* duties, unless otherwise specified, are based on an f.o.b. valuation of imports rather than on a c.i.f. valuation, as in Europe. At given *ad valorem* rates, valuation on an f.o.b. basis, which excludes ocean freight and marine insurance, yields a somewhat lower duty than valuation on a c.i.f. basis, which includes these items. Consequently, to achieve comparability with European tariff averages, the American average should be reduced by roughly 10 per cent (on an unweighted basis, from a level of about 20 per cent for manufactures to a level of about 18 per cent).

[15] So-called because of a 1958 speech in Geneva by Undersecretary of State Dillon, pointing out that under the 1958 renewal of the Reciprocal Trade Agreements program, the United States had authority, expiring in 1962, to offer 20 per cent tariff reductions (with certain exceptions) in exchange for reciprocal concessions. The speech provided the basis for the 1961 GATT tariff negotiations.

It should be noted that the tariff rates reflected in Table 3 are nonpreferential or most-favored-nation rates. In the case of the United Kingdom particularly, and to a smaller degree of France, a large fraction of imports is admitted at much lower preferential rates or entirely free of duty. When the United Kingdom abandoned free trade in the early 1930s, it continued to remain on a virtually free-trade basis with the rest of the British Commonwealth. Even for manufactured goods, protective duties or other trade barriers on products originating in Commonwealth countries are rare; well over nine-tenths of such imports enter the United Kingdom duty-free. Since about 40 per cent of Britain's imports in recent years have been obtained from the rest of the Commonwealth, the observation that the United Kingdom is a high-tariff country must be qualified by the statement that it maintains a preferential policy of virtually free trade on a large fraction of its imports. Similarly, between one-fifth and one-fourth of France's total imports come from the French franc area, and these imports enter France either duty-free or at reduced duties.

Range and Distribution of Tariffs on Manufactured Goods

The tariff information in Table 3 is useful as a first approximation but, in the absence of further knowledge, is entirely inadequate as a measure of national tariff levels. In particular, it tells us nothing about the range and distribution of tariff rates within each country, which, needless to say, can vary widely. To take two cases, a 5 per cent average tariff level in one country might be the result of uniform duties of 5 per cent on all commodities, whereas in another country it might be the result of a tariff schedule in which 90 per cent of the import categories were subject to no duty at all while 10 per cent were subject to protective duties of 50 per cent. Even though an unweighted arithmetic

TABLE 4

Frequency Distribution of Average Duties on Groups of Manufactured Goods in the North Atlantic Countries

	Class 1 0-5%	Class 2 6%-10%	Class 3 11%-15%	Class 4 16%-20%	Class 5 21%-25%	Class 6 26%-30%	Class 7 31%-35%	Class 8 36%-40%	Class 9 41%-
Percentage of total duties in each class									
Benelux	12.2	37.8	26.7	16.7	6.7				
France	2.2	13.3	15.6	33.3	28.9				
Germany	26.7	45.6	21.1	6.7		6.7			
Italy	2.2	5.6	10.0	42.2	26.7	8.9	2.2		2.2
EEC Common Tariff	4.4	18.9	34.4	34.4	5.6	2.2			
Austria	6.7	16.7	12.2	26.7	28.9	7.8	1.1		
Denmark	52.2	26.7	13.3	6.7	1.1				
Norway	22.2	20.0	30.0	15.6	8.9	2.2	1.1		
Portugal	9.6	6.0	13.3	8.4	18.1	4.8	14.5	4.8	20.5
Sweden	30.0	44.4	22.2	2.2		1.1			
Switzerland	30.0	42.2	23.3	2.2	1.1	1.1			
United Kingdom	2.2	10.0	17.8	31.1	28.9	7.8	2.2		
United States	5.6	8.9	22.2	22.2	16.7	7.8	12.2	1.1	3.3

Cumulative percentage

	Class 1 0-5%	Class 2 6%-10%	Class 3 11%-15%	Class 4 16%-20%	Class 5 21%-25%	Class 6 26%-30%	Class 7 31%-35%	Class 8 36%-40%	Class 9 41%-
Benelux	12.2	50.0	76.7	93.4	100.0				
France	2.2	15.5	31.1	64.4	93.3	100.0			
Germany	26.7	72.3	93.4	100.0					
Italy	2.2	7.8	17.8	60.0	86.7	95.6	97.8	97.8	100.0
EEC Common Tariff	4.4	23.3	57.7	92.1	97.7	100.0			
Austria	6.7	23.4	35.6	62.3	91.2	99.0	100.0		
Denmark	52.2	78.9	92.2	98.9	100.0				
Norway	22.2	42.2	72.2	87.8	96.7	98.9	100.0		
Portugal	9.6	15.6	28.9	37.3	55.4	60.2	74.7	79.5	100.0
Sweden	30.0	74.4	96.6	98.8	98.8	100.0			
Switzerland	30.0	72.2	95.5	97.7	98.8	100.0			
United Kingdom	2.2	12.2	30.0	61.1	90.0	97.8	100.0		
United States	5.6	14.5	36.7	58.9	75.6	83.4	95.6	96.7	100.0

Source: See text.

average of all duties would give the same figure in both cases, the economic implications in the first instance would clearly be radically different from those in the second. In the first case the pattern of production and consumption and the level of real income might differ little from the situation under conditions of completely free trade, whereas in the second case the existence of a few important highly protected high-cost industries could change the picture drastically. If we are to make adequate tariff comparisons, it is therefore necessary to have a measure of the range and distribution of tariff rates in the countries being compared.

Information of this nature for North Atlantic countries is provided in Table 4, which presents a frequency distribution of average tariff rates on the 90 categories of manufactured goods in Part I of the PEP study, *Atlantic Tariffs and Trade*. The 90 average tariff rates for each country are grouped into nine class intervals of five percentage points each (except Class 9, which embraces all duties of more than 40 per cent).

A frequency distribution is helpful in revealing a country's tariff structure. Thus, while average tariffs on manufactured goods are somewhat higher in Italy than in France, the most common groups of duties in both countries are in Classes 4 and 5 (with a combined range of duties from 16 to 25 per cent). Sixty-two per cent of all French tariffs and 69 per cent of Italian tariffs fall within this range. In contrast, prior to 1962 the United States had a higher average tariff than either France or Italy, yet the most common tariff groups were Classes 3 and 4 which range from 11 to 20 per cent), the two classes together accounting for 44 per cent of American duties on manufactures. Portuguese tariffs, apart from having by far the highest average, are the most widely and evenly distributed if class intervals of ten percentage points are considered. And curiously, Portugal has more than twice as many duties as the EEC common external tariff in Class 1, where levels range from 0 to 5 per cent.

Denmark, Germany, Sweden, and Switzerland clearly qualify as low-tariff countries. In the case of Denmark, Class 1 is actually the most common category; indeed, over half of Danish duties on manufactured goods are 5 per cent or lower (11 per cent are duty-free). In each of the four countries, between 70 and 80 per cent of all duties are at a level of 10 per cent or lower, and in all four well over 90 per cent of all duties are 15 per cent or lower. By way of contrast, only 18 per cent of Italian duties on manufactures are in the first three classes.

Analysis of Tariffs by Commodities

At this point we should get down to cases. We need to know where in the broad sector of manufactured goods tariffs tend to be particularly high, where they tend to be average, and where they tend to be low. Much of the relevant information is summarized in Table 5, which shows the average duties on each of 90 groups of manufactured goods for the United States, the United Kingdom, and for the EEC common tariff.

TABLE 5

Average Duties on 90 Groups of Manufactured Goods for the United States, the United Kingdom, and the EEC Common Tariff[a]

(In per cent)

	U.S.	U.K.	EEC
Chemical Products			
Inorganic chemicals	14	14	11
Organic chemicals	*33	*27	*15
Tar, crude chemicals from coal, oil, gas	3	10	4

Table 5, *continued*

	U.S.	U.K.	EEC
Coal-tar, dyestuffs, natural indigo	*81	*21	*15
Dyeing, tanning extracts	*33	7½	7
Pigments, paints, varnishes	*26	16	*16
Pharmaceuticals	12	17	*15
Essences; perfume, flavor materials	*27	15	10
Perfumes, cosmetics, soap, cleansers	20	12	*18
Fertilizers, mfd.	2	16	4
Explosives	17	17½	*15
Plastics, primary forms	*25	15	*16
Miscellaneous chemical products	19	11	13
Leather, Furs			
Leather, natural	10	14	9
Leather, reconstituted or artificial	11	10	10
Leather manufactures	17	*20	*16
Furs, dressed or undressed, dyed	*31	*20	14
Rubber Manufactures			
Rubber, fabricated materials	15	14	13
Tires, tubes	19[b]	*27	*21
Other rubber manufactures	19	*22	*18
Wood, Cork Manufactures			
Veneers, plywood, reconstituted wood	11	14½	12½
Other wood manufactures, n.e.s.	19	14	14
Cork manufactures	*24	15	*20
Paper products			
Newsprint paper	0.	0	7
Common packing, wrapping paper	14	15	*18
Other paper, paperboard	12	18	*17
Articles of pulp, paper, paperboard	16	18	*19
Textile Fibers, Fabrics			
Yarn of wool, hair	*25	17	8
Cotton yarn, thread, unbleached	17	16	10
Cotton yarn, thread, bleached, dyed mercerized	14	18	13
Yarn, thread, synthetic or artificial	*32	*24	*17
Other yarn, thread	*22	*21	11
Cotton fabrics, unbleached	*23	*23	*17
Other cotton fabrics of standard type	*25	*23	*17
Woolen, worsted fabrics	*46	*22	*18
Jute fabrics	8	*23	*23
Fabrics of synthetic fibers	*33	*27	*20
Other standard noncotton fabrics	*25	*22	*19

Table 5, *continued*

	U.S.	U.K.	EEC
Tulle, lace, embroidery, ribbons, etc.	*35	*24	*19
Special textiled fabrics	*27	*25	*15
Articles made of textiles, except clothing	*30	*31	*19
Floor coverings, tapestries	*21	*23	*21
Clothing, Footwear			
Clothing, except fur clothing	*32	*26	*19
Fur clothing	*33	*25	*23
Footwear	19	*25	*19
Nonmetallic Mineral Manufactures			
Cement	2	7	8
Other building materials, not glass, clay	14	13	10
Clay, refractory construction materials	20	17	12
Mineral manufactures, n.e.s., excluding clay, glass	20	15	12
Glass	*23	*19	12
Glassware	*35	*21	*20
Pottery	*35	*25	*20
Silver, platinum group metals	*33	7	7
Precious, semi-precious stones, pearls	17	5	3
Jewelry	*36	*21	10
Iron, Steel			
Pig iron, sponge iron, ferro-alloys	9	9	7
Ingots, blooms, slabs, billets, bars	12	11	7
Finished forms of iron, steel	11	14	9
Pipes, fittings, cast	10	17½	13½
Other iron, steel	*21	17	12
Ordnance	*26	*22	11
Metal manufactures, n.e.s.	*23	*21	*16
Machinery			
Power-generating machinery, not electric	15	*19	14
Farm machinery, implements	3	14	11
Tractors, not steam	6	*22	*16
Office machinery	12	16	14
Metalworking machine tools	17	17½	8
Other metalworking machinery	14	*19	13
Conveying, hoisting, excavating, road, mining machinery	12	16	13
Textile machinery	18	18	13
Other industrial machinery	15	17	13

Table 5, *continued*

	U.S.	U.K.	EEC
Electric generators, alternators, motors, transformers, etc.	*23	*24	*15
Other electric machinery, appliances	18	*21	*16
Transport Equipment			
Automobiles	8½	*30	*29
Buses, trucks	10½	*28	*24
Other road motor vehicles	12	*25	*26
Road vehicles other than motor vehicles	18	*22	*19
Aircraft	12½	*19	13½
Railway vehicles	16	*23	13
Ships, boats	7	6	4
Other Manufactured Goods			
Prefabricated buildings, parts	18	9	8
Plumbing, heating, lighting fixtures, fittings	*22	*20	*17
Furniture	*24	*20	*17
Travel goods	*30	18	*20
Scientific apparatus	*28	*33	*17
Photographic supplies	14	17	*17
Watches, clocks	*46	*30	13
Musical instruments, records	20	*25	*17
Printed matter	12	6	10
Manufactured goods, n.e.s.	*24	*20	*15

ᵃ The figures in this table do not take into account the "Dillon round" of tariff reductions negotiated in 1961 under the General Agreement on Tariffs and Trade.

ᵇ 10 per cent if bicycle tubes are excluded.

* An asterisk indicates that the duty is above the average for manufactured goods in the country (or customs area) concerned.

n.e.s., not elsewhere specified.

Source: PEP, *Atlantic Tariffs and Trade, A Report* (London, Allen & Unwin, 1962), Part I.

Perhaps the most obvious conclusion to be derived from Table 5 is that some degree of tariff protection is well-nigh universal in the sector of manufactured goods. Only in the case of one commodity, newsprint paper, does a zero duty appear, and that for only two of the three customs areas. The second conclusion is that higher-than-average duties for each customs area (indicated in the table by an asterisk) tend to cluster in particular commodity groups. Thus, in all three customs areas almost all textile and clothing items have duties higher than average, and the same is true of glassware and pottery. In other sectors, such as nonelectric machinery, iron and steel products, and building materials, duties tend to be lower than average.

In large measure this situation appears to be easily explainable in terms of comparative advantage. On the one hand, such industries as textiles, pottery, and glassware have encountered growing competition from lower-cost producers (such as Japan), and their continued existence depends, or is believed to depend, on a high degree of protection. On the other hand, in such sectors as machinery and steel products, Western Europe and the United States are the low-cost producers of the world and therefore have little need of protective support. Low duties are also frequently found in two other categories. The first group comprises products, such as certain building materials, which enjoy a considerable degree of "natural protection" because of the high cost, in relation to the value of the product, of transporting these items over any substantial distance. The other group includes many "intermediate products" on which, as in the case of industrial raw materials, there is a positive incentive for keeping duties low in order to minimize the cost of manufacturing articles in a later stage of production.

Atlantic Tariffs in Transition

Directly or indirectly because of the Common Market and related developments, the Atlantic tariff structure is rapidly changing. In the first place, tariffs are being removed, many months ahead of schedule, within the European Economic Community and the European Free Trade Association; by the end of 1963 both the Community and the Association had gone 60 per cent of the way toward the complete internal removal of customs duties on non-agricultural products. In the second place, the Common Market external tariff is progressively being established; in mid-1963, two and one-half years before the date prescribed in the Rome Treaty, the Community took the second of three steps in the formation of the common frontier. Finally, under the "Kennedy round" of GATT tariff negotiations (a direct response to the emergence of the Common Market) a determined effort is being made to achieve major "across-the-board" reductions in duties on both sides of the Atlantic.

The eventual level of the Community's common tariff is still far from clear. Under the Rome Treaty the general rule—to which there were many exceptions—was that the duty for each item was to be the unweighted arithmetic average of the duties prevailing on January 1, 1957, in each of the four participating customs areas (Benelux, France, Germany, and Italy). Under this formula, duties in the low-tariff member countries would have had to rise sharply; on the basis of the unweighted tariff averages in Table 3, Benelux tariffs on manufactured goods would have had to rise, on the average, by about 25 per cent, and German tariffs by about 70 per cent.

The first step toward a common tariff took place on January 1, 1961, one year ahead of schedule. In order to make the accelerated timetable more palatable to the low-tariff members, and in anticipation of the "Dillon round" of tariff negotiations, the Community decided to offer other GATT countries a 20 per cent reduction in the common tariff in exchange for reciprocal concessions. The first step in the alignment of duties was therefore made on the assumption of a common tariff 20 per cent below the level contemplated in the Rome Treaty.[16]

Unfortunately, as already noted, the tariff reductions achieved under the Dillon round were, on both sides of the Atlantic, far short of the "linear" 20 per cent target originally proposed. The Community attributed its own failure to approach the target to inadequate reciprocity by other GATT countries. Nevertheless, in its second step toward the formation of a common tariff, the Community again based the prescribed tariff changes on the Rome Treaty formula, less 20 per cent, even where tariff reductions had not been effected under the 1961 GATT Agreement. This liberal rule was retained in anticipation of tariff reductions under the "Kennedy round." The Community has decided, however, that the rule will not apply after 1965 if "adequate" concessions are not received from the "Kennedy round" negotiations.

[16] In this first step national duties which were not more than 15 per cent below the reduced common tariff were raised all the way to the latter level. National duties which were more than 15 per cent below the reduced common tariff were raised by 30 per cent of the difference between the two levels. National duties which were above the original (nonreduced) common tariff were reduced by 30 per cent of the difference between the national level and the reduced common tariff, except where this rule would bring the duty below the level of the original common tariff, which provided a floor for tariff reductions in both the first and second steps.

6

Britain and the Common Market

If Europe united is to be a living force, Britain will have to
play her full part as a member of the European family.

WINSTON CHURCHILL, 1947

Britain, in effect, is insular, maritime, and linked by her trade
—her market and her suppliers—to a great variety of countries, many of which are distant ones. . . . How can it be
brought about that England, as she lives, as she produces,
as she trades, can be incorporated in the Common Market as
it had been conceived and as it functions?

CHARLES DE GAULLE, 1963

Whatever its broader significance, the collapse in January 1963
of the long negotiations for British membership in the European
Economic Community abruptly put an end to the easy optimism
which, until then, had prevailed on both sides of the Atlantic with
respect to the Community's future. For the breakdown reflected a
victory, at least for the time being, of views which either could
wreck the movement toward a united Europe or could mold the
Common Market into a form which would be in the interest
neither of Atlantic strength nor of free world solidarity.

By 1960 it was becoming increasingly clear that, from the
standpoint of Western European and Atlantic cohesion, few
questions deserved higher priority than the relationship of the
United Kingdom to the European Economic Community. Without
Britain, as Churchill had noted long before, no effort toward
European union could escape the charge of being an anomaly;

and it was surely ironic that the Community, as a most ambitious step toward a united Europe, should have had the effect—at least temporarily—of increasing, rather than diminishing, European disunity. The situation which had arisen was one which called for the highest statesmanship not only because the issues were highly complex, but because their repercussions were truly global in scope. For a time it appeared that these issues would be successfully, though far from easily, resolved by bringing Britain into the Common Market as a full member. This hope was crushed by the events of early 1963.

In assessing the blame for these melancholy events, some share must be assigned to the British themselves. For Britain, the emergence of the Community had been a highly disturbing development. In the beginning, as De Gaulle has correctly intimated, the British government regarded the Common Market as a project which it expected, and indeed hoped, would never come to fruition. When this expectation proved to be mistaken, the British, in their long negotiations of 1956-58 for an OEEC free-trade area, made strenuous efforts to have the best of two worlds by attempting to avoid both a political involvement with the Community and the unfavorable commercial consequences of noninvolvement. But their high hopes for these negotiations turned out to be equally unwarranted. Their next strategy was to reach agreement with Austria, Portugal, Switzerland, and the Scandinavian countries on the formation of a new regional arrangement, the European Free Trade Association, a major purpose of which was to negotiate with the Community from a position of strength.

With certain doors closed because of the failure of earlier negotiations, a change in British opinion regarding the Common Market became increasingly evident in late 1960 and early 1961. On the negative side the early acute misgivings in Britain about the Common Market were gradually diminishing, and on the positive side a growing number of Britons were impressed with the political and economic advantages of British membership in the Community, provided the membership fee was not too high. By early 1961 the British government openly indicated that it was engaged in bilateral conversations with the Common Market countries, and in July of that year it announced that it was prepared to explore with the Community the possibility of becoming a full member.

The Case for Joining the Community

With the Community firmly established as a going concern, the case for British membership was indeed very strong. British membership, if coupled with appropriate arrangements for the other excluded Western European countries, would put an end to the economic and political friction which had resulted from the emergence of two large rival regional arrangements and thus would remove a dangerous source of European and Atlantic disunity. More positively, it would enable Britain to increase its influence in Western European affairs, an influence which threatened to diminish if Britain remained outside the Community. Seen in this light, British membership was fully as much a matter of American as of British concern. From an American standpoint British influence was sorely needed in Community affairs because, of all Western European countries, the United Kingdom was the most accustomed to thinking in global terms. In large measure (as De Gaulle noted with disfavor), Britain's political and commercial interests were outside Europe, and its participation in Community decisions would on this account almost certainly be helpful in checking insular tendencies. British political skills, Americans believed, would also be helpful in making the common institutions more effective and in strengthening European democracies.

In addition to these important political considerations, the

United Kingdom had strong economic motives for entering the Common Market. First, such a step would give Britain free access to the market of the Six and thus would achieve, by another route, what the British had tried to attain in their unsuccessful negotiations for an OEEC free-trade area. As time passed, a second and related consideration became at least as important in British thinking. This was the conviction that membership in the Community would give a decided boost to British economic growth by promoting a more rapid increase in industrial productivity, which for years had been lagging far behind that of most major continental countries.[1] Growth and productivity would be stimulated, Britons believed, both by increased exposure to continental industrial competition and by increased access to the flow of investment funds pouring into Western Europe from the United States and other sources. For years Britain had received the lion's share of American investment in Western Europe, but this situation was rapidly changing. As recently as 1957 the United Kingdom had accounted for 57 per cent of the flow of American funds for new direct investment in Europe. By 1959 the figure had dropped to 45 per cent, and by 1962 to 22 per cent. In the meantime, the share of the Common Market countries in the flow of American direct investment to Europe had risen from 36 per cent in 1957 to 49 per cent in 1962.[2]

Of the economic considerations affecting the British decision to join the Common Market, this was probably the most im-

[1] In the United Kingdom, industrial output per worker was 12 per cent higher in 1960 than in 1953. In Belgium the corresponding increase was 19 per cent; in Germany, 34 per cent; in the Netherlands, 40 per cent; in France, 60 per cent; and in Italy, 63 per cent.

[2] The flow of American direct investment is here defined as the sum of the net capital outflow from the United States for direct investment, plus the undistributed earnings of American firms and subsidiaries operating abroad. The percentages above are derived from data in a series of special articles on United States foreign investment in the *Survey of Current Business* (especially September 1960 and the August issues of 1961, 1962, and 1963).

portant. The British feared that if they failed to join, they might within a few years be hopelessly left behind in a race in which, with old and obsolete plants and machinery, they would be confronted with a dynamic United States of Europe which would be continuously retooled with the latest and most efficient industrial equipment. Even to such a skeptic as Hugh Gaitskell, this was a persuasive consideration. In a speech to the House of Commons on June 6, 1962, he declared: "I am not saying the balance of argument is against entry. My view is that probably, in the long run, the economic arguments might be favorable largely because of the attraction of foreign and particularly American investment."

Thus there was a strong case for joining the Community, particularly if this could be accomplished before Community policies had largely congealed. In this situation time was not on the British side. Provided the price of membership was not too high, the sooner the British joined the Community the better, for by joining early they would be in the best position to check those tendencies which were in conflict with their interests.

In the British case, however, there were reasons to fear that the price of membership might be too high. Of these reasons two were of special importance. First, there was the political danger of an erosion of Commonwealth ties—a prospect which, because of its implications for the low-income countries of the Commonwealth, could have serious consequences for the entire free world. Second, there was the economic danger of massive Vinerian trade diversion, particularly in the form of a shift from low-cost Commonwealth sources of temperate zone foodstuffs to high-cost European sources (including, possibly, much greater reliance on United Kingdom food production). One could argue that such trade diversion was a moderate price to pay for membership in the Community, yet it was clearly a cost that would have to be offset against the economic gains in any balance sheet giving a true account of the net impact of British membership.

Thus the choice confronting the British in 1961 could not be simply stated in the alternatives: to join or not to join. Everything depended on the terms of membership, and from the outset it was recognized on both sides of the table that the negotiations at best would be long and difficult, with possibly only an even chance of success. Consequently, apart from the arbitrary manner in which it was induced, the collapse of negotiations in January 1963 could not be regarded as a complete surprise. But this is a story which is far from over. A door has been closed which conceivably may open again at a more favorable time. If and when it does, the same complicated set of interests which prolonged the earlier negotiations will have to be dealt with anew. Indeed, they will have to be dealt with in working out any British *modus vivendi* with the Six. It is important, therefore, to take a closer look at British interests as they relate to the Community.

Britain and the Commonwealth

For geographical and historical reasons British interests are far less centered on Western Europe than are those of the Six. First and foremost, the United Kingdom is leader of the British Commonwealth, a loose association of states in all stages of economic development. Whatever else may be said about the Commonwealth, it accounts for a very substantial proportion of the world's land area and population, the fraction being about one-fourth in each case. It is important to remember that, apart from the dependencies, which have been rapidly declining in number, the Commonwealth is an association of sovereign states having complete freedom both in internal and in international matters. In the words of a British official, "Every one of the member nations enjoys unfettered control of its own affairs. Thus it determines its own foreign, domestic, and fiscal policies; defines its citizenship and immigration regulations; negotiates and signs treaties with other nations; maintains its own diplomatic service; and decides for itself the issues of peace and war. . . . In short, no member of the Commonwealth can dictate to another in any matter whatsoever, nor is any Commonwealth nation under any obligation to underwrite the responsibilities undertaken by any other Commonwealth nation."[3] A high degree of cooperation of course exists on many matters, but it is important to emphasize the independent status of Commonwealth members because, while the United Kingdom can decide its own policies in relation to the European Economic Community, it is in no position to speak for the rest of the Commonwealth. Any general policy for the Commonwealth as a group can be worked out only on the basis of negotiation and general agreement.

The Commonwealth is bound together by commercial and financial ties, but it cannot be evaluated in purely commercial and financial terms. For historic reasons the United Kingdom has a heavy moral responsibility for the welfare particularly of the poorer and less developed members. In view of recent events in the underdeveloped world, notably in Africa, this moral claim is clearly reinforced by the British political interest—fully shared by the United States and other Atlantic partners—in preventing a vast extension of Soviet penetration. Thus, entirely apart from any economic considerations, it would be folly for Britain to turn its back on the Commonwealth.

This does not mean, of course, that British economic interests in the Commonwealth are unimportant. But here the questions become complex and technical, and it will be advisable to distinguish sharply a number of distinct matters which, in discussions in the press and elsewhere, are often mixed together in a

[8] Mimeographed address by J. Brian Cullen, Counsellor to the British Embassy in the United States, September 4, 1959.

most confusing way. First, there is the matter of the overseas Commonwealth as a United Kingdom source of supply, particularly of cheap food; second, there is the matter of the overseas Commonwealth as a market for the United Kingdom; and, third, there is the matter of the United Kingdom as a market for the rest of the Commonwealth. We shall consider each of these three topics in turn, but since all three are in one way or another related to the matter of Commonwealth Preference, we shall first take a quick look at that subject.

Commonwealth Preference

Commercially, the Commonwealth is bound together by a system of largely reciprocal tariff concessions known as Commonwealth Preference (until recent years, the usual label was Imperial Preference). Preferential treatment of Britain's exports by other Commonwealth members has a long history, with Canada introducing preferences in 1898, New Zealand and South Africa in 1903, Australia in 1908, and India in 1927.[4] Until the 1930s, however, there was little scope for reciprocity by the United Kingdom in view of its traditional policy of free trade.[5] This state of affairs abruptly changed when Britain departed from free trade during the depression, for the departure was almost completely confined to countries outside the Commonwealth. With minor exceptions, the new duties applied only to goods from non-Commonwealth sources, and thus the preferences extended by the United Kingdom to the rest of the Commonwealth had by 1937 become fully as

[4] The information in this section is largely derived from the comprehensive article by Sir Donald MacDougall and Rosemary Hutt, "Imperial Preference: A Quantitative Analysis," *Economic Journal*, June 1954, and from the excellent PEP study, *Commonwealth Preference in the United Kingdom* (London: Allen & Unwin, 1960).

[5] The British began to depart from free trade in 1919 with the introduction of the McKenna duties and certain later tariff measures, but the resulting preferences in most cases were unimportant in Commonwealth trade.

important as the preferences extended by the rest of the Commonwealth to the United Kingdom.

Since the late 1930s, Commonwealth Preference has diminished considerably in scope and sharply in degree. In 1937 preferences applied to roughly three-fifths of the trade (in both directions) between the United Kingdom and the Commonwealth, and in both directions the average margin of preference on goods enjoying preference was close to 20 per cent.[6] (On *all* Commonwealth goods, it was about 11 per cent in both directions.) By 1948 the fraction of trade affected by preferences had dropped to about half of Britain's exports to the Commonwealth and to somewhat over half of the Commonwealth's exports to Britain. Moreover, the average margin of preference on goods enjoying preference had dropped to about 15 per cent on Britain's exports to the Commonwealth, and to about 12 per cent on Commonwealth exports to the United Kingdom. (On all Commonwealth goods, including those not subject to preference, the average margin of preference in 1948 was about 7 per cent in both directions.)

This decline in the importance of Commonwealth tariff preferences was partly the result of tariff reductions[7] and partly the result of price increases which reduced the incidence of specific duties. For the same reasons the scope and degree of preference has continued to decline since 1948. In 1957, according to the PEP study, the average margin of preference on all of Britain's

[6] The margin of preference is the difference between the tariff rate applied to non-Commonwealth imports and the tariff rate applied to imports from the Commonwealth. Thus, if the tariff on a given commodity from a source outside the Commonwealth is 20 per cent and if the tariff on the same commodity from the Commonwealth is 5 per cent, the margin of preference is 15 per cent. The averages cited here are weighted averages, the weight given to a commodity corresponding to its relative share in the imports of the country extending preference.

[7] In particular, the tariff reductions obtained in the trade agreement of 1938 between the United States and the United Kingdom and those obtained in the GATT tariff negotiations of 1947.

imports from the Commonwealth was only 4 per cent; on goods enjoying preference (47 per cent of United Kingdom imports from the Commonwealth), the average preference was 9 per cent. However, the scope and degree of preference varied greatly with the type of commodity imported. On raw materials, for example, the average margin of preference on goods enjoying preference was 8 per cent, but since only 27 per cent of such imports enjoyed preference, the average margin of preference on all raw materials imported by the United Kingdom from the Commonwealth was only 2 per cent. In the case of manufactured goods, on the other hand, the average margin of preference on goods enjoying preference was 16 per cent, and since 79 per cent of such imports enjoyed preference, the average preference on all manufactures purchased by Britain from the Commonwealth was 12 per cent.[8]

While recent estimates are not available, the extent of preference on United Kingdom exports to the Commonwealth (about half of which enjoy no preference whatever) has likewise continued to decline. Where they exist, the preferences again vary greatly. They are negligible on United Kingdom exports to Commonwealth countries in tropical Africa, for example, but they continue to be important on exports to such countries as Australia, New Zealand, and Canada.

The British Stake in Cheap Food

For the United Kingdom, the Commonwealth is of particular economic significance as a source of supply. From the Commonwealth,[9] Britain imports almost half its food and almost half its

[8] However, only 8 per cent of Britain's imports from the Commonwealth in 1957 consisted of manufactured goods, whereas 41 per cent consisted of raw materials.

[9] Strictly speaking, the Commonwealth Preference area, since certain countries, such as Eire and the Union of South Africa, participate in the Commonwealth Preference system but are no longer members of the Commonwealth.

raw materials. These imports are entirely free from protective duties,[10] and only a small fraction is subject to revenue duties.[11] In 1957, for example, 90 per cent of Britain's food imports from the Commonwealth were entirely free of duty, the remaining 10 per cent being subject to revenue duties which averaged only about 4 per cent *ad valorem*.[12] In the same year, virtually all of the raw materials imported by the United Kingdom from the Commonwealth were entirely free of duty. Even in the case of manufactured goods, almost all of Britain's imports from the Commonwealth are completely duty-free; in 1957, only 3 per cent were subject to duties of any kind.[13]

Thus, in its relationship to the Commonwealth the United Kingdom behaves, in effect, as a member of a vast virtually free-trade area. For Britain it is an area which far surpasses the Six (or, for that matter, all of Western Europe) as a source of supply. In 1959, for example, 44 per cent of Britain's imports came from the Commonwealth Preference area, whereas only 14 per cent came from the Six.

Britain, as President de Gaulle has rightly stated, "has very little agriculture"; in the late 1950s agriculture accounted for only 5 per cent of total employment in the United Kingdom, compared with a figure of 10 per cent in the United States and 26 per cent in the Six. Thus Britain is exceptionally dependent on outside sources for food, in fact importing more food than any other country in the world. Indeed, if intra-Six food imports are ex-

[10] With the insignificant exception of artificial silk waste.

[11] Revenue duties are those which apply either to goods which the United Kingdom does not produce or to goods which, when produced in the United Kingdom, are subject to an excise duty. The main examples are tea, cocoa, coffee, sugar, alcoholic beverages, and tobacco.

[12] The figures in this paragraph have been derived from Table VIII (p. 17) of the previously cited PEP study, *Commonwealth Preference in the United Kingdom*.

[13] About four-fifths of the duties in this small dutiable sector are protective, with an average incidence of about 20 per cent *ad valorem*.

cluded, Britain imports more food than the six Common Market countries combined, although its population is only about 30 per cent that of the Six. In 1958, for example, United Kingdom food imports were $3.9 billion, compared with net EEC food imports (i.e., imports from outside the Community) of $3.4 billion.

Stating the matter another way, the United Kingdom produces less than half of its food, whereas the Six have produced about 85 per cent of their food requirements in recent years. France, Italy, and the Netherlands are virtually self-sufficient in food production, their deficiencies in some foods being offset by export surpluses in others. Germany and Belgium have substantial food deficits, each country producing about 70 per cent of its food. To a large extent the net food imports of these two countries are supplied by other members of the Six.

Table 6 provides greater detail on agricultural self-sufficiency in the United Kingdom and the Six, showing domestic production of selected food items as a percentage of total requirements (defined as domestic production plus net imports). A figure of less than 100 indicates a deficiency (supplied by net imports) of the item concerned, whereas a figure of more than 100 indicates a surplus (i.e., net exports). With the exception of eggs, fish, and potatoes, the United Kingdom has major deficiencies in all of the food categories listed. In sharp contrast the Six, considered as a group, have a really conspicuous deficit only in fats and oils; and here one must exclude butter, in which they are self-sufficient. Several of the Six have large deficits in particular items, but these deficits are largely met by purchases from others of the Six. Thus, the Italian surplus in fruit, the French surplus in cereals and sugar, and the Dutch surplus in dairy products, vegetables, and fish go a long way to meet deficiencies in these foods in other members of the Community.

The striking difference between the food position of the United Kingdom and that of the Six did much to prolong the negotiations

TABLE 6

Domestic Production of Selected Foods as a Percentage of Total Requirements 1957/58

	United Kingdom	EEC	France	Germany	Italy	Belgium and Lux.	Netherlands
Cereals	50	86	108	75	95	47	36
Bread grain	36	89	105	81	96	61	45
Coarse grain	64	81	112	69	92	39	30
Meat	58	96	99	90	86	95	132
Beef	65	92	99	86	79	95	98
Pork	54	102	101	96	97	101	170
Fish	87	90	94	89	64	59	211
Butter	11	100	104	91	83	95	206
Cheese	52	99	103	78	101	33	205
Eggs	93	90	95	57	86	109	248
Sugar	24	93	107	78	101	109	75
Fats, oils*	17	42	38	31	69	23	34
Vegetables	80	103	98	78	116	101	151
Potatoes	96	102	101	99	98	94	138
Fruits, nuts	32	82	58	51	133	57	72
All food							
Pre-war	30	85	87	80	97	56	96
47/48–49/50	42	85	89	75	94	59	97
56/57–57/58	45	86	94	69	98	69	103

* Excluding butter.
Source: OEEC, *Agricultural and Food Statistics*, Paris, 1959.

on the terms of British entry into the Common Market. In their
earlier unsuccessful efforts to form a free-trade area linked with
the Community, the British had always firmly insisted on excluding both British agriculture and the Commonwealth Preference system from any arrangements toward European integration.
The purpose of these exclusions was, of course, to safeguard both
the British stake in cheap food and the overseas Commonwealth's

preferential access to the United Kingdom market. But the British position in this regard was never acceptable to the French and, for that matter, was never popular with the Dutch or the Italians, whose countries are both major exporters of food products. In any case, on this as on other issues, the Six insisted that if Britain was to join the Community, it must join on the terms of the Rome Treaty, including acceptance of the "common agricultural policy" under which regional protection would replace the national systems of protection previously in effect.

As events have already abundantly illustrated, the adoption of a common agricultural policy was to be a formidable undertaking for the Six themselves but, for the United Kingdom, there were major additional difficulties. First of all, the British protected certain food products by a different system from that used by the Six. In the United Kingdom, protection was effected mainly by a system of direct subsidies to farmers, with tariffs and quotas playing only a modest role. Food imports from the Commonwealth were virtually duty-free, and duties on food imports from other sources averaged only about 8 per cent. Moreover, certain important products, such as wheat, were duty-free from all sources. Thus food prices in Britain were determined under virtually free-market conditions and, in most cases, were at a substantially lower level than those prevailing on the Continent where agriculture, as in the United States, was protected by national systems of price supports implemented by import barriers in the form of quotas or high tariffs.

In the British system the commodities that were subsidized were few but important. They included cereals, livestock, eggs, milk, and potatoes. During the late 1950s, the subsidies averaged close to a half billion dollars annually. Where this method of agricultural protection is exclusively used, the consumer pays the same food prices that he would pay under conditions of completely free trade, and bears the cost of protection in the form of higher taxes. In other words, the impact of protection is not in a higher cost of living but in a higher tax bill. From the economist's point of view, the method of direct subsidies has the great virtue —in contrast to tariffs and quotas—of carrying a price tag. The subsidies paid to farmers are a conspicuous item in the national budget, and the cost of protection is exactly known in dollars and cents.

This said, however, it should be emphasized that from the standpoint of the British consumer, the paramount consideration was not the method of protection but the degree of protection. If the scope and degree of agricultural protection were the same in Britain as in the Six, the British consumer would not have suffered from the change in protective technique.[14] What he would have lost in higher food prices, he would have gained in lower taxes. But it was far from evident that agricultural protection in the Community would be at approximately the same level as it was in the United Kingdom. It is impossible to make a categorical statement on this matter, since the Community has not yet agreed on how much agricultural protection it wants, but the possibility that membership in the Community might involve a sharp net increase in the level of British agricultural protection was far from remote. To see why this was so, it will be helpful, first, to compare the existing degree of agricultural protection in Britain and in the Six and, second, to examine the conflict within the Community between the higher-cost and the lower-cost food producers.

In Table 7 the average prices received by Britain's farmers in 1959-60 are compared with the average prices received by farmers in the Six. The British prices include the direct subsidies paid to farmers. Participation in the Community's common agri-

[14] There might, however, be other disadvantages. For example, a sharp increase in the cost of food, even if accompanied by a tax reduction, might make much more difficult the task of preventing inflationary wage increases.

TABLE 7

Average Price Received by Farmers in Britain and in the EEC for Selected Foodstuffs, July 1959-June 1960
(Cents Per Kilogram)

	U.K.[a]	EEC	Ratio of EEC Price to U.K. Price
Wheat	7.4¢	9.1¢	123.0
Rye	6.0	7.6	126.7
Barley	7.6	7.9	103.9
Oats	7.3	7.7	105.5
Potatoes	3.6	3.8	105.6
Sugar Beets[b]	10.9	10.2	93.6
Beef Cattle[c]	39.8	44.9	112.8
Hogs[c]	20.2	51.3	102.2
Eggs	73.0	64.9	88.9
Butter	98.8	146.0	147.8

[a] Price includes direct subsidies.
[b] Equivalent per kilogram of pure sugar.
[c] Live weight.
Source: PEP, *Agriculture, the Commonwealth, and EEC,* Occasional Paper No. 14, July 1961, Table 2, p. 46.

cultural policy, assuming a continuation of these price relationships, would have required an increase in protection for those commodities of which the British price (including subsidy) is lower than the EEC price. Thus, for most of the commodities in the table an increase in protection would have been dictated, and in several cases a sharp increase. Under the existing pattern of British food consumption the net increase in the cost of British food would have been roughly in the neighborhood of $1 billion a year, involving an increase in the cost of living of about 2 per cent.

But this rather modest estimate rests on the favorable assumption that the EEC common agricultural policy will not involve an increase in agricultural protection within the Community. Such an assumption is almost certainly unduly optimistic. Under the Community's common agricultural policy, regional protection is gradually replacing national protection, but the method of protection is the continental rather than the British method. That is to say, regional price supports are being substituted for national price supports. Under a system of "variable import levies," import barriers within the Community are to be gradually removed, and a common import barrier for each product to be established against the outside world. The effect of these actions will be to establish a uniform price for each farm product within the Community. The degree of protection in each case will, of course, depend on the height of the regional support price, and this is a matter which has not as yet been fully decided.

It would be one thing if these Common Market support prices were set at approximately the average of the national support prices prevailing within the member countries in recent years. In these circumstances the level of agricultural production within the Community might not be significantly affected by the common agricultural policy, the increased production in the lower-cost countries being offset by reduced production in the higher-cost countries. But the assumption that average food prices within the Community will remain where they are may be far from realistic. As Table 8 shows food prices within the Six, prior to implementation of the common agricultural policy, varied widely from country to country. For the products listed, the average price received by farmers in the highest-cost country of the Six was from 30 to 60 per cent higher than in the lowest-cost country. Consequently, if the Community's support price for each product is to be in the neighborhood of the average of the former national support prices, the prices received by farmers in the high-cost countries will in most cases have to fall sharply.

TABLE 8

*Range of Average Prices Received by EEC Farmers
for Selected Foodstuffs, July 1959-June 1960*
(Cents Per Kilogram)

	Lowest-cost EEC Country	Highest-cost EEC Country	Highest EEC Price as Per Cent of Lowest EEC Price
Wheat	7.7¢	10.5¢	136.4
Rye	5.8	9.2	158.6
Barley	6.3	10.1	160.3
Oats	5.9	8.6	145.8
Potatoes	3.2	4.5	140.6
Sugar Beets	1.3	1.9	146.2
Beef Cattle[a]	38.5	51.9	134.8
Hogs[a]	43.7	56.8	130.0
Eggs	47.9	76.6	159.9
Butter	112.0	166.0	148.2

[a] Live weight.
Source: Same as for Table 2.

Unfortunately, in such a situation, the political pressures are far from symmetrical. For while the low-cost producers have little, if any, objection to an increase in support prices, the high-cost producers, as events have abundantly demonstrated, have the strongest objection to a reduction. In these circumstances the Community's support price in each case is likely to be established at a level much closer to the highest, than to the lowest, of the former national price supports.

The British Interest in Cheap Raw Materials

Britain obtains close to half its imports of industrial raw materials from the Commonwealth, and less than one per cent of these are subject to duties of any kind. Duties on raw materials from non-

Commonwealth sources are low, averaging three per cent *ad valorem*, and in some cases are lower than the corresponding duties in the EEC common external tariff.

Like other manufacturing countries highly dependent on foreign markets, the United Kingdom has a major interest in access to cheap raw materials and, because of its precarious balance of payments, is more sensitive to this need than the continental members of the Community. While the EEC common tariff on raw materials in most cases is low, averaging 2.9 per cent, there are a few products on which the duty is much higher than this average. During the negotiations for EEC membership, the British were particularly concerned about the common tariff on a group of basic materials which acquired the label of "the big five." These materials, with their respective EEC common tariffs, were aluminum (10 per cent), lead (8 per cent), zinc (7 per cent), wood pulp (6 per cent), and newsprint (7 per cent).[15] Combined United Kingdom imports of these five commodities averaged $555 million a year in the years 1954-56, with wood pulp alone accounting for $281 million.

Despite strong British efforts at persuasion, the Six declined to agree on the reduction of these common tariffs. In a number of instances, however, the Six provisionally agreed to accommodate British interests by establishing "tariff quotas," as authorized by Article 25 of the Rome Treaty. The tariff quota is a device whereby imports, within stipulated limits, are permitted either duty-free or at reduced duties. As authorized by the Rome treaty, it is an exceedingly flexible instrument. Article 25 sets no time limit on the suspension or reduction of duties, and also sets no limit on the size of the quotas. It merely directs that the Commission

---

[15] The common tariff on lead and zinc is specific, and the figures cited here are approximate *ad valorem* equivalents. These duties were not affected by the "Dillon round" of GATT tariff negotiations concluded in 1962.

"shall periodically examine any tariff quotas granted in application of this Article." Such an examination, it would appear, could be a mere routine formality if the Commission so chose.

If the British negotiations had been successful, the advantage of the tariff quota, from the standpoint of the Six, is that in agreed cases it would have permitted the United Kingdom to extend free trade or preferential treatment to the overseas Commonwealth without requiring the rest of the Community to do so. To provide a situation as acceptable to Britain as the *status quo* such tariff quotas would, of course, have had to be large enough to satisfy the entire United Kingdom demand for the affected products.

While never threatened in the same degree as the interest in cheap food, it is clear that the British interest in cheap raw materials is better served, at least for the time being, by remaining outside the Community.

The Commonwealth as a Market for the United Kingdom

In addition to its importance to Britain as a source of supply of food and raw materials, the Commonwealth has also been of great importance as a market. In fact, as a market for Britain, the Commonwealth has far surpassed the Six. The contrast was particularly noteworthy in the early postwar years. As late as 1951, for example, 51 per cent of Britain's exports went to the Commonwealth, whereas only 10 per cent went to the Common Market countries.

Yet, in their negotiations for EEC membership the British gave every indication of regarding this aspect of the Commonwealth relationship as a matter of secondary importance. Indeed, in the interest of Commonwealth harmony, the United Kingdom negotiators announced that Britain would relinquish its claim to preferential treatment from the rest of the Commonwealth, so that this margin of preference could be used by the overseas Commonwealth in its own bargaining with the Community.

The British attitude was not difficult to explain. As already noted, the scope and degree of Commonwealth Preference have declined sharply during the past two or three decades and, except in one or two cases, remain important only in the high-income countries of the Commonwealth, such as Canada, Australia, and New Zealand. Partly because of the decline of Commonwealth Preference, but mainly because of the rapid economic expansion of Western Europe, the relative importance of the Commonwealth and Western European markets has been slowly but profoundly changing in recent years. Britain's exports to both areas have continued to rise, but at sharply diverging rates. The result has been that from a figure of slightly over half of total United Kingdom exports in 1951, exports to the overseas Commonwealth had by 1961 fallen to only a little over one-third. In the meantime, United Kingdom exports to Western Europe had increased from one-fourth of the total to more than one-third. In sharp contrast to the situation a decade earlier, Britain's exports to Western Europe were almost as large as Britain's exports to the Commonwealth, and there was every indication that the Western European market would shortly surpass the Commonwealth market in importance.

The striking thing about the changing relative importance of the Commonwealth and Western European markets is that tariff developments in the two areas appear to have been of decidedly secondary importance. In 1960 and in 1961, for example, Britain's exports to the Six, where tariff developments were adverse, rose at a considerably higher rate than Britain's exports to EFTA countries, where tariff developments were favorable. The reason, without doubt, was that the spectacular economic expansion in the Six was a more important factor in determining the direction of British exports than the regional tariff changes in the Six and the Seven.

Thus, of the main considerations affecting the British in their negotiations for EEC membership, it is not surprising that the role of the Commonwealth as a United Kingdom market occupied a subordinate position.

The United Kingdom as a Market for the Commonwealth

The United Kingdom as a market for the overseas Commonwealth was a much more troublesome subject in the membership negotiations. Indeed, the problems raised in this connection proved to be among the most intractable of any encountered in the negotiations. For while the threat to British sales in the overseas Commonwealth as a result of joining the Common Market was indirect and even remote, the threat to Commonwealth sales in the United Kingdom was both direct and immediate. The reason was that Britain not only would be abandoning Commonwealth Preference in its purchases from the overseas Commonwealth, but would also be required to establish "reverse preferences" by moving toward free trade with the Community while simultaneously applying against the Commonwealth the EEC common tariff and the common barriers on temperate-zone foodstuffs.

As anyone could have predicted, the reaction of the overseas Commonwealth to these developments was one of acute concern. The United Kingdom had long been a market of paramount importance. In 1959, for example, Britain purchased 56 per cent of New Zealand's exports, 51 per cent of Nigeria's exports, 31 per cent of Ghana's exports, 28 per cent of India's exports, and 27 per cent of Australia's exports. These exports covered a wide range of products: temperate-zone foodstuffs from Australia, Canada, and New Zealand; tropical foodstuffs from Ghana, Nigeria, and India; raw materials from Canada, Australia, and Malaya; and manufactured goods from Canada, India, and Hong Kong.

During the early stages of the negotiations the British hoped that it would not be necessary for Britain to apply the Community's common tariff (and common barriers on foodstuffs) against the overseas Commonwealth. On this matter the interests both of the British consumer and of the overseas Commonwealth producer were clearly in the same direction. Such a solution was not, however, acceptable to the Six, and as a result the British were forced to attempt an accommodation of the interests of the United Kingdom and the Commonwealth by other means. The outcome was a patchwork of provisional compromises, with several important matters still at issue when the negotiations broke down.

In discussing the compromises that were provisionally worked out, it will be useful to distinguish the problems of the low-income Commonwealth countries from those of the high-income countries. Because of their possible impact both on human misery and on the solidarity of the free world, the arrangements affecting the low-income countries were matters of special concern. The British negotiators originally took the position that all of the poorer Commonwealth countries should have the right to form some kind of tie with the Community that would give them duty-free access to the Common Market. However, because of the threat of low-wage industrial competition, particularly in textiles, the Six were unwilling even to consider the association of India, Pakistan, Ceylon, and Hong Kong; and, for its part, India indicated that it did not want a tie with the Community. The Six nevertheless agreed that, with certain exceptions, the British tropical countries, including such newly independent countries as Nigeria, should be invited to apply for association with the Community on the same basis as the original associated overseas territories.

This invitation was coolly received by several of the British tropical countries; but even if it had been accepted by all the countries for which it was intended, it would have done nothing to ease the difficulties of such countries as India. The effect on India of British membership in the Common Market would have been of particular significance, because India, apart from being one of the poorest of nations, accounts for about one-fifth of the population of the non-Communist world. Moreover, in contrast to the situation in most of the other low-income countries of the Commonwealth, a large fraction of Indian exports to the United Kingdom (about one-fourth) are manufactured products—mainly textiles and leather goods.

It cannot be said that the provisional compromises affecting India were particularly satisfactory from an Indian point of view, and it is hardly surprising that the Indians were disturbed about them. In the agreement tentatively reached with the Six the United Kingdom was to apply the EEC common tariff against India but, in the case of cotton textiles, at a somewhat slower rate. If future Indian earnings from such exports were to fall below specified levels, the United Kingdom was to be permitted to take measures—perhaps in the form of tariff quotas—to ease Indian access to the United Kingdom market. These arrangements, such as they were, were hardly an adequate response to Indian difficulties, for if India was to pay for the expanding imports which would accompany the economic expansion it was striving so hard to attain, it would need vigorously growing export markets. Thus the assurance that the new EEC duties on Indian exports to Britain would be temporarily reduced if such exports were to fall to some level specified by the Community was cold comfort indeed.[16]

While the arrangements with the low-income countries might in the long run have more profound implications, the arrangements with the high-income countries played a much more important role in prolonging the negotiations. The main problem in this connection was the treatment of temperate-zone foodstuffs, a matter of interest mainly to Australia, Canada, and New Zealand. The Six insisted that Britain, if it were to become a member of the Community, would be required to participate fully in the common agricultural policy, and they interpreted this to mean that Britain would have to apply against the overseas Commonwealth the common external barriers on foodstuffs. For a time the British negotiators sought a special dispensation in the form of tariff quotas that would have permitted food imports from Australia, Canada, and New Zealand to continue to enter the United Kingdom free of duty. The Six, however, would not agree to this solution, except possibly in the case of New Zealand, which was notably dependent on the United Kingdom market and was recognized by all parties as a special case.

As a long-run approach to these problems, the Six and Britain agreed that a solution should be sought in world-wide commodity agreements. It was provisionally agreed that an international conference, to which all temperate-zone food-producing countries would be invited, should be held at an early date to work out agreements on a wide range of farm products. In view of the breakdown of negotiations, it is perhaps idle to speculate on what the prospects for such a solution would have been. To say

[16] Apart from the tentative agreement on Indian textiles, the United Kingdom was able to obtain provisional agreement to remove the common tariff on certain products. Of these, the most important was tea. In addition, the common tariff was to be removed on spices and on certain minor items, such as cricket bats.

the least, however, it is clear that to work out commodity agreements which would have been acceptable not only to the Six and to Britain, but also to Canada, Australia, New Zealand, Argentina, and the United States, would have been a prodigious achievement.

Britain, the Common Market, and the United States

The failure of Britain to achieve membership in the European Economic Community has been a serious blow not just to Britain and its partners in the European Free Trade Association, but also to the United States. For the latter, British membership would have promoted two important American objectives: first, it would have removed an important source of European disunity by ending the split between the Six and the Seven; and, second, it would have assured that the Community would be an instrument of Western European, rather than of merely "Little European," integration.

The American government had been less sympathetic with earlier British moves toward integration with the Six. In particular, American policy makers were openly cool toward the British attempt in 1956-58 to form a purely commercial link with the Community. During the first postwar decade the United States had acquiesced in a high degree of European trade discrimination as a hopefully temporary necessity imposed by the world dollar shortage. The discrimination involved in the British proposal for a Western European free-trade area had no such rationale and, to the American leadership, appeared as a threat to United States commercial interests unaccompanied by any compensating advantages in the direction of European political union.

In sharp contrast, the British decision to apply for full membership in the European Economic Community was greeted with unconcealed rejoicing in Washington as a step of immense significance in the establishment of a truly united and "outward-look-ing" Europe. This does not mean that British membership in the Community would have been an unmixed blessing for the United States. In recent years, American exports of foodstuffs to the United Kingdom have averaged in value almost half of those going to the Six, and in some years, such as 1960, the fraction has been much greater. British participation in the Community's common agricultural policy would have threatened a large proportion of such exports, and some trade diversion would have also probably occurred in other sectors. But these risks were regarded by the American government as far outweighed by the anticipated benefits of British EEC membership in the form of increased Western European and Atlantic solidarity.

For the time being, these considerations have been academic. As noted earlier, however, the final chapters of this story remain to be written. While President de Gaulle has certainly altered the timing of the Community's development, it is by no means clear that he has significantly affected the eventual outcome.

7

The Common Market and the
Poor Nations

If we are to face the vast gap between the rich nations and
the poor, between the nations round the Atlantic area which
have been through their modernizing revolutions and the
searching nations all around the world who seek desperately
to make the same transition, perhaps the first decision we
have to make is to abandon the fallacy that somewhere,
somehow, everything is going to turn out all right. We have
to be ready to be as foresighted, as determined, as ready to
work and to go on working, as our busy Communist com-
rades. We must be prepared to match them policy for policy,
vision for vision, ideal for ideal.

BARBARA WARD, 1962

In terms of population the great bulk of the non-Communist
world consists of countries which, by any standard, must be
described as poor—in many cases, desperately poor. As Professor
Tinbergen has written, "we must realize that most of the people
in Asia and Africa and many in Latin America are living at a
starvation level. Their consumption is some 10 per cent of that
in developed countries and they are in a constant fight against
hunger and illness. Everything in their budget—food, clothing,
housing, education, amusement—is far below adequate standards
as we see them."[1] Just where one should draw the line between

[1] Jan Tinbergen, *Shaping the World Economy: Suggestions for an International Economic Policy* (New York: The Twentieth Century Fund, 1962),
p. 10.

the poorer countries and the richer countries is a matter of judgment, but if we somewhat arbitrarily designate the poor nations as those having an average annual income per capita of less than $350, about two-thirds of the inhabitants of the free world would be included in this category.[2] Thus defined, the poor nations would embrace all of Asia except Japan, all of Africa except southern Africa, and most of Latin America.

The poverty of these countries is reflected in many ways, some of which do not easily lend themselves to measurement. Much, however, is grimly revealed in two related statistical series. Almost without exception, infant mortality in these countries is high and life expectancy low. In 1958-59, 14.6 per cent of all babies born in rural India (excluding stillbirths) died before they were a year old. For the Dominican Republic (as a whole), the corresponding figure in 1960 was 11.4 per cent; for Ghana, 11.3 per cent; for Guatemala, 9.2 per cent; and for Mexico, 7.4 per cent. In the richer countries the story is very different. In the United States, for example, only about 2.5 per cent of all babies die during their first year, and for some countries, such as Sweden and the Netherlands, the figure is less than 2 per cent. Partly because of high infant mortality, but also because of high death rates at other ages, life expectancy is much lower in the poor countries than in the rich. Thus the life expectancy of a male child at birth, which in the United States and in most of Western Europe is in the neighborhood of 70 years, is only 33 years in Haiti, 41 years in Burma, and 45 years in India.[3]

[2] The fraction is roughly the same for the Communist world.

[3] This black picture has been changing in recent years as death rates have declined with the introduction of modern low-cost methods of disease control. Unfortunately, the fall in death rates has not been an unmixed blessing, since it has not been accompanied by a corresponding decline in birth rates. As a result, population in many low-income countries is growing at rates of 2 to 4 per cent a year—rates which greatly limit the possibilities for alleviating human misery. For a searching study of this problem, see Ansley J. Coale and

Apart from being poor, many of these countries have only very recently acquired national independence. As former colonies of Western European powers they are inclined—understandably if not always too reasonably—to regard their present economic difficulties as mainly the result of a long history of colonial exploitation. Because of their poverty, their political inexperience, and their frequently bitter feelings about their colonial past, these countries are particularly vulnerable to the appeal of communism —a fact which, of course, has by no means been overlooked by the Communist leadership.

The moral should be painfully obvious: in determining its foreign economic policies the United States, because of its weight in the world economy, must be sensitive to the problems and aspirations of the poorer nations if the free world is to have a promising future. This proposition is highly pertinent to the relationship of the United States to the Common Market. Here there are two problems. The first is a widely recognized but rather narrow problem involving discrimination by the Common Market countries in their imports of tropical products. A much broader and more important problem concerns the relationship, within the free world, of the richer countries toward the poorer countries—a relationship in which the rich nations have not, as yet, squarely faced certain serious matters arising out of their trade policies with the poor nations. As we shall see, the problems of the low-income countries in the field of trade have a profound bearing on the forms which Atlantic cooperation (particularly in the commercial sector) should—and should not—assume. Before expanding on this theme, however, it will be useful to deal first with the narrower problem of Common Market commercial discrimination in tropical products.

Edgar M. Hoover, *Population Growth and Economic Development in Low-Income Countries* (Princeton: Princeton University Press, 1958).

The Problem of Discrimination in Tropical Products

In the Treaty of Rome the signatory countries agreed to free their trade not only among themselves, but also with their overseas dependencies, most of which are in tropical Africa. These "associated overseas territories," many of which have recently become independent nations, are outstanding as producers of tropical primary products, and their prospective free access to the Common Market has been a source of deep concern to those tropical countries not having a link with the Community.

The Rome Treaty prescribes that member states are to apply to the associated overseas territories the same rules for the removal of tariffs (and quantitative restrictions) that apply to themselves. For a given member of the Community, the major significance of this provision will be with respect to the associated territories of the other members. Thus France, which already extends free trade to its own associated territories, will in a series of stages be applying the same policy to designated overseas countries having "special relations" with Belgium, Italy, and the Netherlands.

For the associated territories, the tariff rules laid down by the treaty are somewhat less strict than those applying to the European members. Associated territories may "levy customs duties which correspond to the needs of their development . . . or which, being of a fiscal nature, have the object of contributing to their budgets."[4] They are thus able to employ tariffs within the Community both to protect infant industries and to raise revenue. The only restriction is that such duties should, within the transition period, be made nondiscriminatory within the Community. For this purpose the timing and targets which are specified for the European member states in their projected removal of tariffs within the Community apply, in the case of an associated terri-

[4] Article 133, paragraph 3.

tory, merely to the removal of the tariff preferences accorded to the European member with which it has "special relations."

In any case, it is not the prospective trade measures of the associated territories toward the Community which worry the tropical countries that have no link with the Common Market but, rather, the prospective measures of the Community toward the associated territories. Specifically, the tropical countries of Latin America and non-EEC Africa fear that, because of emerging tariff discrimination, their exports of primary products to the Community will in large measure be replaced by exports from the associated territories.

If the Six were of minor importance as a market to the non-EEC tropical countries, the matter could perhaps be regarded as of secondary concern. But the opposite is true. Before the emergence of discrimination, about one-fifth of the exports of Latin America, and about one-third of the exports of Ghana and Nigeria, went to the Common Market countries.

The principal exports threatened are coffee, sugar, cocoa, and bananas. In each case the Community originally planned to impose a substantial common external tariff. For coffee, the tariff was to be 16 per cent; for sugar, 80 per cent; for cocoa beans, 9 per cent; and for bananas, 20 per cent. It is clear that at these rates Latin American and non-EEC African exports would have encountered a degree of discrimination ranging from moderate in the case of cocoa to extreme in the case of sugar.

For numerous reasons, it is far from easy to estimate how seriously the prospective discrimination will threaten the exports of non-EEC tropical countries. Many variables are involved, and the ultimate level of the Community's common tariff on the affected products has not been firmly decided. For our purposes it will be necessary to rely on the informed, but far from confident, guesses of the commodity experts. These appear to agree that, under the originally scheduled tariff rates, the threat of trade diversion would have been serious in each of the four main tropical products and that, in view of the low "income elasticity" of demand for these commodities, the losses from trade diversion would not have been quickly offset by sales attributable to the Community's rising level of income.

Fortunately, the Community has become increasingly aware of this threat and has undertaken a number of remedial measures. Thus the common external tariff on coffee has been provisionally reduced from 16 to 9.6 per cent and on cocoa from 9 to 5.4 per cent, a reduction in each case by two-fifths. The common tariff on tea, which was originally set at 35 per cent and later was reduced to 18 per cent, has been completely suspended. While this concession is of minor interest to Latin America and Africa, which produce little tea, it is of great interest to India, the most populous and among the poorest of the non-Communist nations. The common tariff on tropical woods has also been suspended. These actions have sharply reduced the originally contemplated degree of discrimination, and offer the hope of further moves in the same direction.

But there is another important way in which the Community can help the low-income countries, both those which are linked with the Common Market and those which are not. In Europe tropical products have long been a favorite source of government revenue—a source tapped not only by tariffs but also by high internal taxes. On coffee, for example, Germany, at the time the Rome Treaty went into effect, imposed a 25 per cent import duty plus a 47 per cent excise tax; France imposed a 20 per cent duty plus a 51 per cent excise; and Italy imposed a 7 per cent duty plus a 66 per cent internal tax.[5] Thus, in each of the three countries the combined impact of the two taxes was over 70 per cent

[5] *Trends in International Trade: Report by a Panel of Experts* (Geneva: The Contracting Parties to the General Agreement on Tariffs and Trade, 1958), p. 106.

ad valorem. Both the tariff and the excise tax were obviously purely revenue measures for Germany, since it neither produces coffee domestically nor has any associated territories.

This habit of obtaining revenue from taxes on products which are the means of livelihood of a large group of the poorer nations of the wold is unfortunate. In the 1960s, moreover, it is a conspicuous anachronism. In a partial attack on the problem President Kennedy in 1961 proposed that the United States and the Community jointly maintain a policy of free trade in those tropical products where no important domestic production is involved. Although this proposal, which is incorporated in the Trade Expansion Act of 1962, is specifically directed to customs duties, it clearly applies in spirit to excise taxes as well. For the United States the Kennedy proposal would merely preserve the *status quo* with respect to the four main tropical foodstuffs. Bananas, cocoa beans, and coffee already enter the United States free of duty and are not subject to special internal taxes, while sugar, which is subject both to a duty and to an import quota, is a commodity in which the United States and several Common Market countries have an important domestic producing interest. For the Community, however, the policy would require removal of the common external tariff on coffee, cocoa, and bananas; and, to be of maximum benefit, it would also require removal of internal taxes (which, we have seen, are in some cases much higher than the corresponding import duties).

The Broader Trade Problem of the Low-Income Countries

It would be a serious mistake, however, to assume that the problems of the low-income countries would be largely solved by free trade in tropical commodities or even by free trade in the whole range of primary products. For while the tropical countries will, of course, continue to be the source of such tropical products as bananas, coffee, and cocoa, and while the poorer countries as a group will continue to rely heavily on exports of industrial raw materials, the future of the low-income nations is far from bright if a vigorous expansion of exports in other sectors is precluded.

To understand why this is so, it will be useful to try to look at the problems of the poorer countries from their own point of view. Although the low-income countries are an exceedingly heterogeneous group of nations which vary greatly in size, natural resources, climate, population density, and other characteristics, they all have one objective in common: very understandably, they all want to radically improve their economic position; in the modern idiom, they want to achieve a higher rate of economic growth. And unless the poor nations are able to achieve and maintain an average rate of economic growth per capita at least equal to that of the rich nations, the economic gulf between the rich countries and the poor will grow even greater than it is now. Indeed, as Gunnar Myrdal and others have pointed out, this gulf actually has been widening in recent decades; the rich nations have been improving their lot at a more rapid rate than the poor nations, with the result that inequality in the distribution of world income has tended steadily to increase.

This is a situation which clearly needs correction if the non-Communist world is to offer an attractive future to its less fortunate members. Happily, with help from the richer countries, an increasing number of low-income countries are beginning to achieve encouraging rates of economic growth. As a by-product, however, this growth entails a continuous expansion of imports —an expansion which in the case of most of the low-income countries is, in percentage terms, as great as, or greater than, the expansion of income. But if imports in these countries are steadily to expand, they will have to be paid for; and, unless the inflow of foreign aid and of private capital grows at a much higher rate than there is any reason to expect, the expanding imports will have to be paid for mainly by a vigorous and continuous expansion of exports.

The matter may best be understood by examining the figures for a recent year. In 1961, for example, the combined merchandise imports of the low-income countries of the free world amounted to an even $30 billion. Other payment items, such as imports of services and interest installments on loans from abroad, required another several billion dollars of foreign exchange. In the same year the inflow of foreign aid (including assistance received from international and regional organizations) amounted to well under $6 billion, or to less than one-fifth of the amount needed to pay for imports.

Another $3 billion of foreign exchange was provided by the net inflow of private long-term capital.[6] But while foreign aid to the low-income countries has in recent years revealed a strong upward trend, no such trend has been apparent in the flow of private long-term capital, which since the mid-1950s has remained in the neighborhood of $3 billion a year. Of this, the great bulk goes to countries with extractive industries. For those low-income countries not endowed with profitable opportunities for investment in petroleum or mining, private capital from abroad has with few exceptions been of very limited significance indeed, whether considered from the standpoint of its contribution to economic development or to the balance of payments. To cite a particularly striking, if somewhat extreme, comparison: the total value of American direct investments in India, which has a population of over 450 million, is less than $200 million; whereas in Venezuela, with a population or less than 8 million

[6] The figures for aid and private investment are from *The Flow of Financial Resources to Developing Countries in 1961* (Paris: Organization for Economic Cooperation and Development, 1963).

—but with abundant oil—the value of such investments is $2.8 billion.[7]

Actually, by far the most important source of foreign exchange for the low-income countries is the flow of earnings from merchandise exports, which in 1961 amounted to $27 billion. Thus it is clear that, unless the rich nations are prepared to contemplate an enormous expansion in foreign aid, the expanding imports accompanying healthy rates of economic growth in the poor nations will require a vigorous and sustained growth of exports.

Here, however, the prospects are far from encouraging. In the past the poor nations have mainly been exporters of primary products. These products fall into two broad categories, crude foodstuffs and industrial raw materials. Both groups will, of course, continue to find a market in the richer countries, but in each case the prospects for a vigorous expansion of sales are by no means bright.

The outlook is particularly unencouraging in the case of foodstuffs. For these, the "income elasticity" of demand in the richer countries is low. That is to say, as income in the rich countries expands, the demand for food also expands, but at a much lower rate. This state of affairs is well illustrated in the case of the United States. During the interwar period, a ten per cent increase in American income was accompanied by only about a four per cent increase in American imports of crude foodstuffs. In technical jargon, the income elasticity of demand was about 0.4. Since World War II—perhaps mainly because American per capita income is at a much higher level than during the interwar years— this coefficient appears to have settled at an even lower figure; during the 1950s, it was in the neighborhood of 0.3.

Such a situation is typical not only of the United States, but of

[7] *Survey of Current Business,* August 1963, p. 18.

the high-income countries as a group. The moral, of course, is plain: even under conditions of free trade in tropical foodstuffs, as the American administration has proposed, the low-income countries could not expect a sustained expansion of sales in this sector that would be commensurate with import requirements under conditions of vigorous economic growth.

In the case of industrial raw materials the prospects are perhaps brighter, yet they are far from reassuring. One might assume that the demand for raw materials within the industrialized countries would vary more or less proportionately with the level of industrial production, and this assumption would doubtless be reasonable if other factors remained constant. In recent decades, however, "other factors" have been of immense importance. Developments in synthetic materials (notably in artificial textile fibers, such as rayon and nylon, as well as in artificial rubber and in plastics) have greatly reduced the dependence on foreign sources for a growing number of raw materials that were formerly highly important in international trade. Moreover, in certain industries, such as electronics, great economies have been achieved in the use of imported raw materials. The result of these developments in the case of the United States has been that, since the war, imports of industrial raw materials, adjusted for price changes, have been rising only about half as rapidly as industrial production.

Thus, neither in the sector of foodstuffs nor in the sector of raw materials is the outlook bright in the low-income countries for a vigorous expansion of exports. This means that, if the needed expansion is to occur, exports of primary products will have to be supplemented by expanding sales of manufactured goods.

To some extent, of course, this has already been happening. For example, Latin American exports of manufactured goods to

Western Europe (OEEC countries) rose from 3.8 per cent of total Latin American exports to that region in 1951 to 7.3 per cent of a considerably larger total in 1958. For the African countries associated with continental OEEC countries, the corresponding figures in the same years were 2.5 per cent and 7.3 per cent. While for most of the low-income countries, manufactures are still a small percentage of total exports, there are conspicuous exceptions. About one-fourth of India's exports to the United Kingdom are manufactured goods (mainly textiles and leather goods), and almost all of Hong Kong's exports to the United Kingdom (96 per cent in 1957) are manufactures—notably textile fabrics and clothing.

The Problem of "Low-Wage" Goods

But here we come face to face with a problem of major dimensions. As the low-income countries gradually become competitive in certain types of manufactured goods, say textiles, their exports encounter increasing trade barriers (however euphemistically these are labelled) in the high-income countries, which are highly sensitive to competition in the form of "low-wage" or "cheap-labor" goods.

Almost by definition, the low-income nations are characterized by low wage rates. In Guatemala, for example, the average hourly wage rate in manufacturing is only about one-seventh the corresponding wage rate in the United States, and for certain other low-income countries the fraction is even lower than this. Far from indicating that the low-income countries as a group are highly competitive in the industrial sector, the low wage rates— as everyone who has taken a course in elementary economics knows—are a reflection of low productivity (that is, of low output per worker) and of a situation in which the labor cost per unit of output may be as high as, or higher than, in the high-income countries.

Yet the matter cannot be left here. For with the introduction of modern capital equipment in the low-income countries, the low wage rates may make it possible for the developing countries to undersell the high-income nations in certain types of manufactured goods. Thus, if markets remain open, there may be a considerable expansion in exports of manufactures. And such an expansion, as we have seen, is a necessity if the poorer countries are to pay for the imports which will accompany a healthy rate of economic growth. This is a fact of life which may for a time be concealed by foreign aid or by wishful thinking, but it can be ignored only at the free world's peril.

For some time the American approach to the problem has been to ask Japan and Hong Kong, for example, to place "voluntary" quotas on their exports of textiles; and there has been much agitation, on one pretext or another, to raise the already high American tariff on textile products. While externally imposed export quotas make it possible for the United States to give the appearance of a liberal trade policy in this sector (apart, that is, from the high tariff), the economic effect is of course exactly the same as would result from the imposition of American import quotas on the same products. From an American point of view, this is simply a method of brushing the problem under the rug.

Implications for European and Atlantic Integration

The problem of low-wage goods is bound to lead to increasing friction and frustration within the free world as the low-income countries industrialize unless the high-income countries are able radically to alter their point of view. Moreover, the problem has a profound bearing on the manner in which the United States should relate itself to regional arrangements such as the Common

139

Market, the European Free Trade Association, or the proposal for an "Atlantic Free Trade Area."

For the time being, of course, there is no early prospect of American participation in an Atlantic free-trade arrangement. Indeed, in view of the implacable opposition of President de Gaulle, the subject would appear to be highly academic. Even before De Gaulle's celebrated press conference of January 1963, however, President Kennedy had made it abundantly clear that there was no intention on the part of the American government of seeking membership in an expanded Common Market or Atlantic Economic Community. Undoubtedly this position was at least partly based on the conviction that, during the birth pangs of the Common Market, any such overture was highly premature.

Apart from considerations of timing and expediency, however, there is one very important reason why the United States should never become a member of an exclusive Atlantic free-trade zone. The reason is this: it surely would not be wise or right for the United States, as leader of the non-Communist world, to move toward free trade with the richer countries while retaining protection against the poorer countries. If, for example, the United States were eventually to become a member of the European Economic Community, it would of course have to levy against nonmembers the Community's common external tariff; and the nonmembers, with only a few exceptions, would be low-income countries. Even if the Common Market tariff were considerably lower than it is scheduled to be, such a move would seriously threaten free world solidarity and would greatly intensify the feeling within the poorer countries that the Common Market is simply a "rich man's club."

Nor would the matter be essentially different if the United States were to affiliate with the Community not as a member of the Common Market customs union, but as a member of an

Atlantic free-trade area embracing the European Economic Community, the European Free Trade Association, and perhaps other "Atlantic" countries. For, in this situation as in the first, the United States would be moving toward free trade with the high-income nations while retaining protection against countries, most of which would be in the low-income group.

This, of course, is a purely negative conclusion, prescribing what the United States should not do in its relationship with European regional free-trade arrangements. What the United States *should* do is another question, which will be considered at a later stage since it requires an examination of the interests of the free world as a whole.

8

European Integration and American Exports

United States support for European integration and for the European Economic Community has deep roots. It springs from a recollection of our own federal experience and from a desire to end the sanguinary rivalry that once divided the great states of Western Europe. But Americans have recognized that the commercial manifestation of the Community —the Common Market—implies a substantial degree of discrimination against American trade. Of necessity, it will require adjustments for the industry, agriculture, and labor of the United States and of non-member third countries.

GEORGE W. BALL, 1962

For Americans no judgment of regional developments in Western Europe is complete which fails to examine the effects of these developments on American trade, particularly on American exports. The principal fear in this connection, as Under Secretary Ball has indicated, is that the discriminatory tariff changes associated with the European Economic Community and the European Free Trade Association may be a major deterrent to American sales to the Western European market, a market which in the early 1960s accounted for one-third of all United States exports of nonmilitary merchandise, and well over one-third of all exports not financed by American aid. In academic terms, it is a fear of serious "trade diversion"—a matter which must be of concern not only because of a precarious balance of payments but, more basically, because trade diversion, to the extent that it occurs, involves a less efficient use of economic resources on both sides of the Atlantic.

But trade diversion is not the only effect of European integration on American exports. Against the unfavorable effect resulting from the discriminatory tariff changes must be offset the favorable effect arising from the economic growth of the Community and the Association. To the extent that integration promotes economic expansion, the Six and the Seven may be expected steadily to expand their purchases from the outside world. On balance, therefore, the effect of European integration on American exports could be either favorable or unfavorable, depending on whether the impact of trade diversion were less important, or more important, than the impact of economic expansion.

Apart from these two commonly cited influences, there is another influence that is frequently overlooked. It should be recalled that tariff discrimination within the Community and the Association first emerged at a time when a much more stringent form of Western European trade discrimination, achieved by highly discriminatory import quotas, was rapidly diminishing. The first years of the two regional groups were thus probably characterized, on balance, by a reduction rather than an increase in import discrimination against the outside world. This was especially the case in relation to the United States, for it was against the Dollar Area that European quota discrimination was mainly directed.

During the first years of the Community and the Association it was possible, at best, to make only informed guesses about how these influences would affect American exports. By the end of 1963,[1] however, both the Six and the Seven had gone 60 per cent of the way toward removing internal duties, and the Six had

[1] By mid-1963 in the case of the Community.

taken two of the three steps toward establishing a common external tariff. There is, therefore, some experience that can be analyzed, and it has become possible to derive fairly solid conclusions about matters which, not long ago, were still in the realm of speculation.

An Over-all View

The broad pattern of EEC and EFTA imports from member and nonmember countries is shown in Table 9. Since the introduction of tariff discrimination, both the Community and the Association have been obtaining a somewhat larger proportion of their total imports from their own members. Thus in 1958, the last year before the emergence of EEC tariff discrimination, the Community obtained 29.6 per cent of its imports from EEC countries. This figure has risen in each subsequent year, and in 1963 stood at 38.5 per cent. To a smaller extent, a similar situation has prevailed in the Association. In 1959, the last year before the emergence of EFTA tariff discrimination, the Association obtained 16.2 per cent of its imports from EFTA countries. The percentage remained the same in 1960 but has risen slightly in each subsequent year climbing to 18.0 per cent in 1963.

These trends are sometimes cited as proof of trade diversion—as proof, that is to say, of a shift of imports from nonmember to member sources. No such inference, however, can properly be drawn. Although increased reliance on imports from other members of a customs union or free-trade area can be the result of trade diversion, it can also be the result of "trade creation"—that is, of a shift of purchases from domestic to regional sources. For example, if France, as a result of its tariff reductions within the Community, obtains from other Common Market countries a commodity that it formerly produced itself (or relies more heavily than formerly on imports from other members than on

TABLE 9

EEC and EFTA Imports from Members and Non-members, 1958-63

	1958	1959	1960	1961	1962	1963[a]
EEC imports ($ million)	22,951	24,212	29,613	32,155	35,718	39,216
From EEC countries	6,787	8,089	10,134	11,697	13,395	15,098
From non-EEC countries	16,164	16,123	19,479	20,458	22,323	24,118
From United States	2,802	2,494	3,827	4,053	4,455	4,961
From elsewhere	13,362	13,629	15,652	16,405	17,868	19,157
EEC imports (% composition)	100.0	100.0	100.0	100.0	100.0	100.0
From EEC countries	29.6	33.4	34.2	36.4	37.5	38.5
From non-EEC countries	70.4	66.6	65.8	63.6	62.5	61.5
From United States	12.2	10.3	12.9	12.6	12.5	12.7
From elsewhere	58.2	56.3	52.9	51.0	50.0	48.8
EFTA imports ($ million)		20,016	23,081	23,541	24,602	25,706
From EFTA countries		3,242	3,731	4,050	4,339	4,632
From non-EFTA countries		16,774	19,350	19,491	20,263	21,074
From United States		1,845	2,641	2,373	2,376	2,336
From elsewhere		14,929	16,709	17,118	17,887	18,738
EFTA imports (% composition)		100.0	100.0	100.0	100.0	100.0
From EFTA countries		16.2	16.2	17.2	17.6	18.0
From non-EFTA countries		83.8	83.8	82.8	82.4	82.0
From United States		9.2	11.4	10.1	9.7	9.1
From elsewhere		74.6	72.4	72.7	72.7	72.9

[a] First three quarters at annual rate.
Source: Organization for Economic Cooperation and Development.

145

home production), the share of total French imports that is derived from the Community will rise, even if no trade diversion—no shift of imports from nonmember to member sources—has occurred. Consequently, in the absence of evidence from other quarters, it cannot be assumed that a rise in the fraction of imports obtained from member sources is mainly or even largely a reflection of trade diversion.

Actually, as Table 9 shows, EEC and EFTA imports from both member and nonmember countries have risen sharply since the late 1950s. The relative increase has, of course, been greater with respect to imports from members. In the case of the Community, imports from member countries have more than doubled since the introduction of tariff discrimination. At the same time, Community imports from nonmember sources have expanded briskly, and were 49 per cent higher in 1963 than in 1958, the year before the initial EEC tariff changes. The increase in Common Market imports from the United States has been particularly marked—from $2.8 billion in 1958 to $5.0 billion in 1963, an increase of 77 per cent.[2] Moreover, despite substantial tariff discrimination, the share of EEC imports obtained from the United States in 1963 (12.7 per cent) was slightly higher than the share in 1958 (12.2 per cent).

Although the rates of increase have been less spectacular, EFTA

---

[2] The decline from 1958 to 1959 in EEC imports from the United States is entirely unrelated to Common Market tariff changes. This decline, amounting to $308 million, is not fully confirmed by United States export figures to the Six, which reveal a drop of only $36 million. Actually, in two broad categories—foodstuffs and manufactured goods—American exports to the Six rose sharply in 1959, the rise being slightly outweighed by a drop in exports of industrial raw materials. The reduction in exports of raw materials is explained mainly by two items: a $91 million drop in exports of cotton and a $136 million drop in exports of coal. In neither case was EEC tariff discrimination a cause, since cotton enters the Common Market countries free of duty or other restriction, while imports of coal are under the supervision of the Coal and Steel Community.

imports from both member and nonmember countries have risen sharply since the introduction of tariff discrimination in 1960. In 1963, imports from members were 43 per cent higher than in 1959, whereas imports from nonmembers were 26 per cent higher. Imports from the United States shared fully in the latter rise; the Association's imports from the United States rose from $1.8 billion in 1959 to $2.3 billion in 1963, an increase of 27 per cent. In spite of the preferential tariff changes, the share of total EFTA imports obtained from the United States in 1963 (9.1 per cent) was approximately the same as the share in 1959 (9.2 per cent).

From these figures it is difficult to escape the conclusion that trade diversion issuing from the Six and the Seven—if, on balance, it has occurred at all—has been of minor dimensions, at least in relation to the United States. This conclusion is strongly supported by United States export figures. If trade diversion had been the dominant influence on American exports to the Community and the Association since the introduction of tariff discrimination, the outcome should have been, not necessarily an absolute decline in such exports, but certainly a decline in the fraction of total exports flowing to the two regional groups. Yet this has not happened. In 1959, the year before the first EFTA tariff discrimination, American exports to the Seven accounted for 9.8 per cent of all American exports; in 1963, when United States exports to all areas were one-third higher than in 1959, the share going to the Seven was the same as in the earlier year, 9.8 per cent. Similarly, in 1958, the year before the initial EEC tariff preferences, the Community accounted for 15.3 per cent of all American exports; in 1963, the figure instead of falling had risen to 18.7 per cent.

These statistics refer to United States exports as a whole, including commodities which either have not been subjected to tariff discrimination or would not be expected to be sensitive to moderate tariff changes. To delve more deeply, it will be helpful to examine the major commodity categories: foodstuffs, industrial raw materials, and manufactured goods.

The Special Position of Foodstuffs

In recent years American exports of foodstuffs and tobacco to the Six and the Seven have substantially exceeded an annual total of $1 billion.[3] During the six-year period 1958-63, such exports accounted for about one-fourth of all American exports to the two regional groups, the fraction varying considerably from year to year because of weather and crop conditions. In some years the Community has been a more important market than the Association; in others, the situation has been reversed. For the period as a whole, however, the Community has accounted for 55 per cent of American food and tobacco exports to the two areas. The major food exports to the EEC and EFTA countries are shown in Table 10.

In considering the impact of European integration on United States exports of foodstuffs, it is necessary to distinguish sharply between exports to the Six and exports to the Seven since, in the latter case, the agricultural sector was specifically excluded from the move toward regional free trade.[4] In the case of the Com-

[4] The way was left open, however, for bilateral agreements on particular products. A number of these have been negotiated, notably with Britain, which has been under pressure to accommodate agricultural interests in other EFTA countries. For example, in a bilateral arrangment with Denmark, Britain agreed to suspend its tariff on butter for the duration of the existing quota system, and also agreed to the reciprocal elimination of duties on certain other farm products.

[3] For the period 1958-63 the annual totals, with exports to the Community in parentheses, are as follows: 1958, $914 million ($453 million); 1959, $1,091 million ($566 million); 1960, $1,099 million ($527 million); 1961, $1,199 million ($685 million); 1962, $1,349 million ($786 million); 1963, $1,314 million ($792 million).

TABLE 10

United States Exports of Foodstuffs and Tobacco to the Six and the Seven, 1962
(Millions of Dollars)

	To the Six	To the Seven	To Both Groups	Exports to Both Groups as % of Exports to All Areas
Vegetable foodstuffs	574.9	349.2	924.1	32.7%
Grains	408.0	237.6	645.6	31.5
Corn and products	228.7	169.1	397.8	60.4
Wheat and products	30.8	50.6	81.4	7.6
Other	148.5	17.9	166.4	50.6
Fodders and feeds	61.9	15.3	77.2	54.9
Fruits and products	66.7	62.2	128.9	45.1
Other	38.3	34.1	72.4	20.7
Animal foodstuffs	84.6	66.1	150.7	44.1
Meat products	70.6	21.6	92.2	60.7
Poultry	48.7	7.2	55.9	78.4
Other	21.9	14.4	36.3	45.0
Edible oils, fats	2.2	32.7	34.9	82.3
Other	11.8	11.8	23.6	16.0
Tobacco and products	127.0	147.0	274.0	50.3
Total	786.5	562.3	1,348.8	36.9

Source: U. S. Department of Commerce.

munity, however, the situation is radically different. Agriculture is very much a part of the Common Market, but prediction is exceedingly difficult because of uncertainty about the future degree of agricultural protection.

149

One prediction, however, can be made with complete certainty: the food sector will continue to be characterized by controlled markets—markets in which tariffs, if not entirely replaced by other trade barriers, will frequently be of secondary importance as a method, and therefore highly unreliable as a measure, of protection. The retention of controlled markets might be thought to simplify the problem of prediction, and this would be true if agricultural policies within the Community could be depended upon to have about the same impact on external sources of supply as the systems of control which they will replace. Unfortunately, there is no such assurance. On the contrary, there is a very real danger that member countries, in their efforts to reach agreement on troublesome issues, will find it expedient to come to terms with one another at the expense of outside parties.

As part of the Community's "common agricultural policy," it has been agreed that regional protection should gradually replace existing national protection and that, as a result, the prices received by farmers for the principal agricultural products should eventually be uniform (after allowing for transportation costs) throughout the Community. For most food products these prices will be above world prices, and the difference will be maintained by import barriers of one kind or another. In this connection, the Community intends to rely heavily on the "variable import levy" —a highly flexible device by which imports can be restricted to any desired degree.

Clearly, a great deal depends on the levels at which the Community establishes internal food prices. To take a specific case that has attracted much attention, the price of wheat received by farmers in Germany has in recent years been about 30 per cent higher than the price received by French farmers. Naturally, the German farmer would like the German price for wheat to continue at its existing high level. Under the EEC common agricultural policy, however, a uniform price for wheat would prevail throughout the Community; and a price at or near the German price would greatly stimulate wheat production in the lower-cost countries of the Community, such as France, at the expense of outside suppliers, such as the United States. Although the French consumer can be depended upon to take a dim view of a rise in the price of bread, the French farmer has no objection to receiving a higher price for wheat. In these circumstances, there is likely to be a distinct tendency for the high-cost country—in this instance, Germany—to have its way, at least to the extent of achieving a regional price which, on balance, stimulates production within the Community and reduces purchases from outside.

But general agreement on Community food prices has thus far been impossible to achieve, and the lack of agreement has, in fact, threatened the very existence of the Common Market. Meanwhile, matters have proceeded, in the main, very much as if there were no common agricultural policy. Consequently, there is no evidence that the Common Market has as yet involved substantial trade diversion in foodstuffs. The threat to future American food exports, however, cannot be lightly dismissed.

The official American position on this matter has been that EEC farm policies should be pursued in a way that permits the United States to retain its "historic share" as a source of food for the Common Market countries. This is a reasonable position on the assumption that relative efficiency in the production of foodstuffs remains unchanged in the United States and in the Community. Thus qualified, in fact, the position is simply another way of saying that the United States is opposed to an increase in Common Market agricultural protection.

It is possible, of course, that the American "historic share" as a source of food for the Six might decline in the future because of an increase in the Community's agricultural productivity relative to agricultural productivity in the United States. Actually, agricultural efficiency, whether measured in terms of output per man-hour or output per acre, has in recent years been rising rapidly both in the United States and in Western Europe, and the leadership of the Community hopes to accelerate this development. If, in the years ahead, agricultural efficiency should increase more rapidly in the Community than in the United States, the Community would be expected to produce a larger fraction (and the United States a smaller fraction) of Common Market food requirements. But such a change in the pattern of comparative cost presumably would be accompanied by a reduction in Common Market agricultural protection—that is to say, by a decline in internal Community food prices in relation to food prices in the United States. This outcome, though clearly conceivable, does not appear to be imminent. In the meantime, as we have seen, the pressures would seem to be strongly in the opposite direction.

Outlook for Exports of Industrial Materials

A substantial proportion (28 per cent in 1958-63) of American exports to the Six and the Seven are basic industrial materials, such as cotton, oilseeds, wood pulp, and metals. The Six have been a much more important market for these commodities than the Seven, accounting in 1958-63 for about three-fourths of American sales to the two regional groups.[5] In 1963 such exports totaled $1.4 billion and comprised 39 per cent of United States exports of basic materials to all areas. The major raw-material

[5] For the period 1958-63 the annual totals, with exports to the Community in parentheses, are as follows: 1958, $1,301 million ($957 million); 1959, $1,090 million ($789 million); 1960, $1,845 million ($1,297 million); 1961, $1,535 million ($1,115 million); 1962, $1,287 million ($951 million); 1963, $1,425 million ($1,064 million).

exports to the Community and the Association are shown in Table 11.

TABLE 11

United States Exports of Basic Industrial Materials to the Six and the Seven, 1962
(Millions of Dollars)

	To the Six	To the Seven	To Both Groups	Exports to Both Groups as % of Exports to All Areas
Metals	214.4	95.8	310.2	42.9
Iron, steel raw materials	41.5	1.1	42.6	21.3
Nonferrous metals	172.9	94.7	267.6	53.3
Copper	101.6	40.9	142.5	65.2
Aluminum	39.2	26.4	65.6	43.2
Nickel	5.9	8.2	14.1	51.6
Other	26.2	19.2	45.4	43.4
Oilseeds	174.0	46.2	220.2	51.4
Coal	154.5	10.9	165.4	42.9
Cotton, unmanufactured	111.6	50.9	162.5	30.2
Rubber[a]	62.1	19.6	81.7	43.2
Paper base stocks	50.5	30.0	80.5	47.5
Wood, lumber	27.5	7.1	34.6	24.2
Other basic materials	156.2	75.3	231.5	
Total	950.8	335.8	1,286.6	35.8

[a] Natural and synthetic, excluding rubber manufactures.
Source: U. S. Department of Commerce.

In this sector, as noted in Chapter 5, tariffs and other trade barriers tend to be low or entirely absent, since the ability to compete in international markets to a large extent depends on access to cheap raw materials. Thus, such important materials as cotton, oilseeds, and copper enter both the Six and the Seven at duties not exceeding one per cent, and the Community's common external tariff on all three items is to be zero. Combined American sales of these three commodities to the Community and the Association amounted to $525 million in 1962, accounting for 41 per cent of United States raw-material exports to the two regional groups.

The EEC common tariff will also be zero on unwrought nickel and tin, all metal ores, nontropical hardwoods, most softwoods, and rubber in primary form, both natural and synthetic. In most cases these items also enter EFTA countries either duty-free or at very low duties.

The pressures toward free trade in this sector are illustrated by the Community's resort to tariff quotas in certain cases where the common tariff is to be above zero. For example, although the common tariff on wood pulp is to be 6 per cent, Common Market members have been authorized until 1967 to use duty-free tariff quotas to meet all their requirements. Similarly, aluminum is to have a common tariff of 10 per cent, but Germany and the Benelux countries, which together account for about four-fifths of the Community's imports of aluminum from non-EEC sources, have been authorized to import the metal, under tariff quota, at a duty of 5 per cent. Tariff quotas can be established or prolonged at will by the Community's governing bodies, and thus are a highly flexible technique for achieving a greater degree of freedom of trade than the common tariff prescribes.

American exports of raw materials fluctuate considerably from year to year, but largely in response to changes in the level of industrial production abroad. Trade diversion does not appear to have been of significant dimensions and, in contrast to prospects in the food sector, is not an imminent threat. On balance, indeed, there can be little doubt that the Community and the Association, by stimulating Western European industrial production, have had, and will continue to have, a favorable effect on American raw-material exports.

Outlook for Exports of Manufactures

About half (49 per cent in 1958-63) of American exports to the Six and the Seven can be broadly classified as manufactured goods. As the list of such commodities is very long, embracing many hundreds of individual products, only the major categories are shown in Table 12.

It is in this important sector that tariffs play their chief role. In agriculture, as we have seen, customs duties are frequently of secondary importance as a method of protection; and, because they are usually low or entirely absent, tariffs are in most cases of minor importance in the raw-material sector. For manufactured goods, however, not only is a substantial degree of tariff protection the rule but, with few exceptions, tariffs are the only form of protection now employed in the Community and the Association.

Unlike most foodstuffs and raw materials, manufactured goods are highly "differentiated" products and, even within the narrowest commodity classifications, there may be important qualitative distinctions. Where the qualitative factor is paramount, a moderate tariff may not have much effect on trade patterns; the strong preference for a particular type of American aircraft or bulldozer or electronic computer may make the tariff a minor consideration. On the other hand, where qualitative differences and consumer preferences are less important, even a low tariff—or a low degree of tariff discrimination—may seriously deflect trade.

Whatever the reasons, tariff developments in the Community and the Association have thus far not prevented a remarkably vigorous expansion of American exports of manufactures to the

TABLE 12

United States Exports of Manufactured Goods[a]
to the Six and the Seven, 1962
(Millions of Dollars)

	To the Six	To the Seven	To Both Groups	Exports to Both Groups as % of Exports to All Areas[b]
Machinery and vehicles	976.1	523.9	1,500.0	19.2
Machinery	790.3	419.0	1,209.3	24.9
Electrical	142.6	79.2	221.8	24.2
Non-electrical	647.7	339.8	987.5	25.1
Vehicles	185.8	104.9	290.7	9.9
Autos, trucks, buses	67.7	48.5	116.2	9.5
Aircraft, civilian	108.1	50.3	158.4	46.2
Other	10.0	6.1	16.1	8.1
Chemicals	389.8	168.8	558.6	31.5
Textile manufactures	109.6	60.2	169.8	24.6
Petroleum products	59.0	42.2	101.2	22.9
Paper and products	42.7	40.2	82.9	28.8
Steel mill products	42.6	20.2	62.8	14.4
Metal manufactures	40.6	21.6	62.2	13.7
Other manufactures	182.0	158.6	340.6	
Total	1,842.4	1,035.7	2,878.1	

[a] As defined in footnote 12 of Chapter 5.
[b] Excluding "special category" exports, for which country totals are not published.
Source: U. S. Department of Commerce.

two regional groups. At $3.2 billion in 1963, such exports were exactly twice as high as the $1.6 billion figure for 1958, the last year before the emergence of Western European tariff discrimination.[6] The annual rate of increase between these two years has, however, been far from uniform. As Table 13 shows, a 7 per cent rise in 1959 was followed by a 59 per cent increase in 1960, a negligible rise the next year, then a 6 per cent rise, and in 1963 a 10 per cent increase. The spectacular rise in 1960 is largely explained by two influences: strong boom conditions in Western Europe and (for technological rather than for economic reasons) a heavy concentration in that year of deliveries of American jet aircraft. If we omit 1960, the growth pattern shows no clear trend—in particular, no clear indication that growing tariff discrimination is tending to restrict American exports of manufactures. The same generalization appears to be valid if we consider the Community and the Association separately. In each case (again excluding 1960) the year in which American exports of manufactures have shown the greatest growth since the emergence of tariff preferences is 1963, when such discrimination was at the highest level thus far reached.[7]

These somewhat surprising findings call for a number of comments. The first observation is that tariff discrimination has been introduced very gradually, usually in 10 per cent stages; indeed, the early tariff preferences (those introduced, say, during 1959 and 1960) can only be described as negligible.[8] A 10 per cent internal reduction of a duty as high as 15 per cent *ad valorem* involves a maximum price differential, at the wholesale level, of only 1.5 per cent. Such a modest price advantage, even if none of it is absorbed by the exporter, is not likely to make much of an

[6] As Table 13 shows, American exports of manufactures to countries other than the Six and the Seven were only 19 per cent higher in 1963 than in 1958.

[7] It should be remembered that tariff discrimination in the Association did not commence until 1960.

[8] Moreover, in the case of the Community, the first internal tariff reductions were extended to the United States and other non-EEC GATT countries in those instances where the duty would not be brought below the level originally prescribed for the EEC common external tariff.

TABLE 13

United States Exports of Manufactured Goods to the Six, the Seven, and the Rest of the World, 1958-63
(Millions of Dollars)

	1958	1959	1960	1961	1962	1963	1963 as % of 1958
To the Six:	985.5	1,005.0	1,580.4	1,701.5	1,842.4	2,028.2	205.8
Machinery and vehicles	432.1	420.7	781.3	863.6	976.1	1,011.1	234.0
Chemicals	248.2	282.1	365.7	383.7	389.8	411.7	165.9
Other manufactures	305.2	302.2	433.4	454.2	476.5	605.4	198.3
To the Seven:	607.2	704.5	1,129.6	1,010.1	1,035.7	1,150.6	189.5
Machinery and vehicles	253.1	294.3	543.2	496.0	523.9	532.6	210.4
Chemicals	103.5	129.3	167.3	158.0	168.8	202.7	195.8
Other manufactures	250.6	280.9	419.1	356.1	343.0	415.3	165.8
To the Six and the Seven:	1,592.7	1,709.5	2,710.0	2,711.6	2,878.1	3,178.8	199.6
Machinery and vehicles	685.2	715.0	1,324.5	1,359.6	1,500.0	1,543.7	225.3
Chemicals	351.7	411.4	533.0	541.7	558.6	614.4	174.7
Other manufactures	555.8	583.1	852.5	810.3	819.5	1,020.7	183.6

	1958	1959	1960	1961	1962	1963	1963 as % of 1958
Annual percentage increase in U.S. exports of manufactured goods							
To the Six		2.0%	57.3%	7.7%	8.3%	10.1%	205.8
To the Seven		16.0	60.3	—10.6	2.5	11.1	189.5
To the Six and the Seven		7.3	58.5	0.1	6.1	10.4	199.6
To the rest of the world		—3.6	6.9	1.2	5.8	7.5	118.7
EEC and EFTA cumulative internal tariff cuts as of mid-year							
Tariff cuts in EEC	0%	10%	20%	30%	50%	60%	
Tariff cuts in EFTA	0	0	20	30	40	50	

Source: U.S. Department of Commerce.

159

impression on exports of such items as capital equipment and jet aircraft, where the qualitative factor is of major importance. Moreover, as noted earlier in the chapter, the initial tariff discrimination occurred against a background of diminishing Western European discrimination in the application of import quotas. As late as 1960, the effects of emerging tariff preferences were probably outweighed by the effects of reduced quota discrimination.

This is no longer true, however, and in the meantime tariff reductions within the Community and the Association have passed the half-way mark. Yet United States exports of manufactures to the Six and the Seven have continued to rise at a vigorous, if uneven, rate. Undoubtedly, the principal explanation has been the brisk rate of economic expansion in both regional groups. Exports of capital equipment and chemicals, which (with vehicles) accounted in 1958-63 for about 70 per cent of American exports of manufactures to the Six and the Seven, are mainly determined by the level of industrial production in those regions. Of the remaining exports, a large fraction consists of consumer goods, sales of which are closely geared to the level of Western European income.[9]

Whether the Six and the Seven will continue to be a flourishing market for American manufactured products remains to be seen. Conceivably, American sales in the years immediately ahead will continue to grow at about the same high average rate as that prevailing since the Community and the Association commenced operations. But it would be unwise to take such an optimistic

[9] According to a recent study, the average "income elasticity" of demand for American products in Western Europe is 0.9, which means that, if other influences are held constant, a rise in Western European income is accompanied by an almost proportionate rise in imports from the United States. Rudolf R. Rhomberg and Lorette Boissonneault, "Effects of Income and Price Changes on the U. S. Balance of Payments," *Staff Papers*, International Monetary Fund, March 1964, p. 66.

conclusion for granted. In the first place, it is entirely possible that the remaining scheduled increases in tariff discrimination, which in the aggregate are far from negligible, will have a much more restrictive effect on American sales rather than the quite moderate *net* discrimination that has thus far occurred. In the second place, the outlook could alter sharply if, as is far from improbable, economic growth in the Six and the Seven should proceed at a substantially slower pace. Consequently, although recent experience has been encouraging, the United States is fully justified in its efforts to negotiate the greatest possible reduction in the tariff discrimination imposed against nonmembers by the Community and the Association. But this matter has aspects which go beyond the prospects for American exports, and to these broader aspects we now turn.

9

European Integration and American Trade Policy

> Let it not be said of this Atlantic generation that we left ideals and visions to the past, nor purpose and determination to our adversaries. We have come too far, we have sacrificed too much, to disdain the future now.
>
> JOHN FITZGERALD KENNEDY, 1963

Whatever its effect on the American economy, the European Economic Community has already had a major impact on the foreign economic policy of the United States in the passage of the justly acclaimed Trade Expansion Act of 1962. Unfortunately, the premises on which that Act came into being have, to say the least, been called into question as a result of the statements and actions of President de Gaulle in early 1963, and a re-examination of the direction and focus of American policy, particularly in matters of trade, is therefore in order. Such a review will be attempted in this closing chapter. Because of the far from clear pattern of the Community's future evolution, the task will not be easy, but it will be simplified by concentrating on the primary issues.

The Logic of American Policy

It should first be emphasized that American policy toward European integration has been at least as much influenced by political as by economic considerations. Consequently, any policy conclusions on European integration which rest solely on economic grounds are open to the valid charge of missing the point. For, despite the threat to its international economic position, the United States since the early days of the Marshall Plan has, under a bipartisan policy, strongly supported the cause of European integration, at first in the interest of European recovery and, later, in the interest of European political unity and economic strength. The hope was that these objectives, if realized, would make Western Europe an effective partner in promoting a promising future for the free world.

From the outset, moreover, the United States has consciously accepted the commercially discriminatory implications of European integration. In the early postwar years the United States acquiesced in a strictly intra-European attack on trade barriers, because the dollar shortage appeared to rule out a global attack. The disappearance of the dollar shortage removed this basis for a regional approach in Western Europe, but the emergence of the European Economic Community introduced a new set of considerations in which political judgments were dominant—on both sides of the Atlantic. From a European viewpoint the importance of political considerations can be seen even in what at first sight might seem a strictly economic exercise: the steps taken by the Community to form a customs union. In the thinking of the Community's founders, political objectives were of major significance both in the internal removal of tariffs and in the establishment of a common external tariff. Internally, tariffs and other obstacles to the free movement of goods, labor, and capital were to be removed not only to increase economic efficiency, but also to bind or "cement" the member countries more firmly together politically; externally, the formation of a common tariff wall—whatever its economic rationale—likewise was to serve a political function as a symbol of the geographical limits of this unity.

In terms of geographical scope, unfortunately, the Community could hardly be regarded as an ideal instrument of European integration since it embraced only the "Little Europe" of the Six. Nevertheless, the United States—again on political grounds—vigorously supported the Six as the nucleus of what it hoped would eventually be a much broader grouping that would include most or all of Western Europe, and that might ultimately become an Atlantic or even a Free World Community. On this ground the American government, despite the possibility of adverse economic consequences, strongly encouraged Great Britain in its effort to become a full member of the Community. And it hoped that British membership would shortly be followed by similar arrangements for other EFTA countries, thus ending the unfortunate division of Western Europe into two large rival regional blocs.

With this pattern of evolution in mind, Congress in 1962 courageously passed the Trade Expansion Act under which bold reciprocal tariff cuts, apart from safeguarding American access to the Common Market, would perform the same "cementing" function for the Atlantic Partnership that reciprocal tariff reductions within the Six were performing for the European Economic Community. In addition to the general authorization to cut duties in half, authority to move all the way to free trade was granted for certain product categories, one of which could have been of great importance if Britain had been permitted to join the Community.

American Policy and De Gaulle

Unluckily, this creative response to the "Common Market challenge" almost immediately received a grave blow at the hand of President de Gaulle, who made it clear in January 1963 that his objection to British membership was based on grounds that were diametrically opposed to the American conception of the Community's role in the free world. These grounds were primarily political rather than economic. In his celebrated press conference the French President indicated that he opposed British membership because of his fear that it would open the door to a "colossal Atlantic community" which not only would include, but would be dominated by, the United States. Against this conception of the Community's future development, De Gaulle, from his earliest writing on European unification, had made it abundantly clear that he regarded the role of a united Europe to be that of a "third force"—dominated by France, independent of "Anglo-American" ties, and prepared to pursue policies detached from those of the two giant nations through which postwar conflict has been polarized.[1]

Though the future is clouded, two matters seem clear. First, after a period of considerable uncertainty in 1963, the European Economic Community appears to be here to stay; and, second, it is dominated for the time being by a leader who has a conception of its role very different from that held either by its founding fathers (including, notably, that other great Frenchman, Jean Monnet) or by the many Americans who have placed so much hope in its future. More specifically, the Community is led by a man who has no interest in lowering trade barriers as a means of "cementing" an Atlantic Partnership and who appears to be

[1] Referring to the period 1944-46 and to opinions which date back to 1940, De Gaulle has written: "I intended to guarantee France primacy in western Europe by preventing the rise of a new Reich that might again threaten its safety; to cooperate with East and West and, if need be, contract the necessary alliances on one side or the other without ever accepting any kind of dependency; . . . to persuade the states along the Rhine, the Alps, and the Pyrenees to form a political, economic, and strategic bloc; to establish this organization as one of the three world powers and, should it become necessary, as the arbiter between the Soviet and Anglo-American camps. Since 1940, my every word and act had been dedicated to establishing these possibilities; now that France was on her feet again, I tried to realize them." Charles de Gaulle, *War Memoirs: Salvation, 1944-1946* (London: Weidenfeld and Nicolson, 1960), pp. 178-179.

equally unimpressed by any other reasons for significantly reducing the Community's level of external protection.

This does not necessarily mean, of course, that the French President will be permanently able to alter the direction of the Community's development. Conceivably, after an interruption in the timetable, the Community will resume the pattern of evolution contemplated by its major architects. In the meantime, however, the major attack on Atlantic trade barriers envisaged in the Trade Expansion Act may be virtually paralyzed unless certain questions are squarely faced.

The Basic Question

The central question which must first be answered is whether a bold move toward free trade remains a compelling American objective in spite of the abrupt calling into question of the political assumptions underlying the Trade Expansion Act. Here the author can only state, then attempt to support, his own strong conviction that, entirely apart from political considerations involving the future course of European integration, a drastic move toward American free trade has long been overdue.

The reasons can be compactly stated. The first, though least important, consideration is that the economic case for American protectionism, such as it is, has long since disappeared. The case was first made—and made with great skill—by Alexander Hamilton in his celebrated *Report on Manufactures* of 1791. This carefully argued report is well worth a thorough reading, if only because it reveals how different the conditions of eighteenth century America were from those of today.

Hamilton's views strikingly foreshadow the preoccupations of many a developing country of the 1960s. His basic concern was that, in the absence of protection, the United States might be doomed to remain an agricultural country, precariously—and perhaps permanently—dependent on Europe for its supplies of manufactured goods. Like many leaders in developing countries today, Hamilton was impressed with the instability of agricultural export earnings, which he attributed not only to "natural causes" but also to foreign "artificial impediments"—a phrase which recalls that the problems of farmers have a long history.

Hamilton is an early champion of what most economists would regard as by far the most important and respectable economic argument for protection, namely, the "infant-industry" argument. Briefly, the argument is that protection may be temporarily justified in cases where a country, with the help of such protection, may be able to establish industries which are potentially efficient and fully competitive but which are unlikely to get started without initial assistance in the form of tariffs or subsidies. Within its assumptions, the infant-industry argument provides a straightforward case for protection, but only for temporary protection. As Hamilton observed, the retention of protection "on manufactures long established must almost always be of questionable policy, because a presumption would arise in every such case that there were natural and inherent impediments to success." Protection, that is to say, is justified on infant-industry grounds only in those cases where production is eventually in a position to be profitable on a free-trade basis, and is to be discontinued when no longer necessary.

The Hamiltonian case, then, applies pre-eminently to developing countries, such as the United States in its earlier years and the less developed countries of today. It provides no support whatever for American protectionism in the 1960s, and those who invoke Hamilton in support of the existing American tariff clearly have no understanding of his logic. But this is essentially a negative argument, which one can accept without proceeding to the difficult political judgment that the United States should undertake a vigorous move toward free trade. For the author, the latter judgment is derived mainly from two additional considerations.

In the first place, in spite of years of whittling away at the American tariff, the United States, as shown in Chapter 5, clearly remains among the high-tariff countries. In view of the American position of leadership in the free world, this situation can only be described as an anomaly without any valid excuse. The situation is deplorable particularly because it is abundantly clear that protectionism on the part of the United States and other high-income countries is bound to cause increasing frustration within the free world as the low-income countries gradually become more competitive in manufacturing. If this problem is taken seriously, as it must be if the United States is not, in President Kennedy's phrase, to "disdain the future," it is difficult to escape the conclusion that the "cementing" function of tariff reduction is at least as important in relation to the low-income countries as it is in relation to our Atlantic partners.

In the second place, if the United States attaches a high priority to its own economic strength and economic growth—a priority dictated by considerations both of security and of economic welfare—it can ill afford the luxury of protecting high-cost production. In this connection it is necessary to separate the basic economic argument from those which are essentially peripheral. In enlisting support for the Trade Expansion Act the Administration made its economic case largely in terms of the favorable effect of reciprocal tariff cuts on the American balance of payments and on the number of American "jobs." Official statistical studies reached the conclusion that the mutual lowering of trade barriers would increase American exports more than it would increase American imports, thus reducing or removing the pressure on the balance of payments. At the same time the increased exports, it was concluded, would create more jobs for American workers than the increased imports would replace, thus yielding a net increase in employment. While these conclusions may have been correct and, moreover, may have been important in achieving support for the new legislation, they had little bearing on the basic economic case for tariff removal, which is concerned with the more fundamental consideration of economic efficiency.

At the risk of offending those who have successfully weathered a respectable course in elementary economics, it may be briefly stated that the primary economic argument for freer trade—an argument which applies unequivocally to all developed countries —is that the reduction or removal of trade barriers would increase economic efficiency by promoting a transfer of economic resources from less efficient to more efficient employment. The case is most easily understood, and in fact is strongest, where the move toward free trade is jointly undertaken by a substantial number of countries. In these circumstances labor and capital would move from high-cost industries, previously sheltered by tariffs from foreign competition, to more efficient employment in the export industries now enjoying increased orders from abroad. The result of such a transfer of resources would be an average increase in output per worker and thus, at a given level of employment, an increase in production.

How much efficiency would increase would depend on the initial degree of protection, on the degree to which protection was reduced and, last though not least, on the number of countries participating in the move toward free trade. Since the American tariff is high, a vigorous move toward free trade would doubtless yield major benefits in increased economic efficiency, particularly if the move, as contemplated in the Trade Expansion Act, is jointly undertaken with other countries. For while it can be shown that the United States could gain economically from unilateral tariff reduction, it would stand to gain much more from a multilateral effort embracing Western Europe and other high-income areas. The reason for this is that a multilateral attack on tariffs would make possible a higher degree of international specialization and thus, for each participating country, a more productive use of economic resources. Moreover, because of the increased demand from abroad, each country could remove tariffs with less fear of a net reduction in employment.

The latter point is important because, as experience has amply demonstrated, unemployment and freedom of trade are implacable enemies. It was mass unemployment which brought free trade in Britain to an end three decades ago—the clamor for protection, in the last analysis, being a clamor for jobs. Thus, while only confusion can result from arguing that tariff reduction tends to increase employment—an argument that could not possibly apply to every country undertaking a joint move toward free trade—it is likewise folly to overlook the necessity of insuring that any move toward free trade be combined with adequate safeguards to maintain the level of employment.

But this is not just a matter of tariffs. What is clearly needed are policies to assure a labor market that is adequate to absorb all workers released from less efficient activity, whether their former jobs were in high-cost production sheltered by tariffs or in production that has become high-cost because of advances in technology. The problem, in other words, is to maintain an economy which is continuously able to take full advantage of the increased efficiency made possible both through greater freedom of trade and through never-ceasing innovation. But this is a problem which, with present knowledge, can be effectively dealt with provided sufficient attention is given to two needs: first, the need for adequate facilities to retrain workers released from less efficient employment and, second, the need for maintaining a high level of demand.

The Question of Method

So much for the central question of whether a vigorous move toward free trade remains a compelling American objective. Subject to the foregoing qualifications, this question has been answered emphatically in the affirmative.

But how may the objective best be achieved? If a major breakthrough in American policy is to be achieved and sustained, this second question merits as much consideration as the first, for the answer is far from obvious. The immediate task, of course, is to make as much progress as possible under the Trade Expansion Act and, in particular, to bring the "Kennedy round" of tariff negotiations to a successful conclusion. At the same time two points should be emphasized. The first is that, in view of recent developments within the European Economic Community, it will be difficult even with the most skillful negotiating to achieve anything approaching the steep across-the-board reductions in Atlantic tariffs contemplated in the Trade Expansion Act. The second point is that, whether the negotiations are disappointing or notably successful, the results will fall far short of what is needed if the conclusions of this chapter are accepted. To achieve significant further progress, however, it will be necessary not only to expand American authority to reduce tariffs—an objective which could be achieved by amending the Trade Expansion Act —but also to consider whether existing ground rules provide an adequate basis for a major new attack on trade barriers. In particular, it will be important to re-examine two basic premises of American commercial policy: the premise that trade concessions should be reciprocal and the premise that trade concessions should be nondiscriminatory.

These two principles have long been cornerstones of American policy. Both were embedded in the Reciprocal Trade Agreements program; both, with strong American support, were incorporated into the General Agreement on Tariffs and Trade; and both underlie the Trade Expansion Act of 1962. Any attack on these policies must therefore be regarded as bearing the burden of proof. Nevertheless, in a world in which, under existing procedures, one industrial country can be in a position to block an effective multilateral program of tariff reduction, the question must at least be raised whether reciprocity and equal treatment should be retained as working principles.

With respect to reciprocity, it is difficult to escape the conclusion that the American position is basically right. As we have seen, the case for a multilateral attack on trade barriers is much stronger, both on political and on economic grounds, than is the case for a unilateral attack. The same arguments which strongly support a bold American move toward free trade apply with equal force to other high-income countries; and, further, the economic benefits for the United States—or for any other individual country—would be much greater from a multilateral than from a unilateral effort. Thus, the position that tariff concessions should be reciprocal is entirely reasonable. Reciprocity, indeed, is a *sine qua non* of any multilateral program of tariff reduction, and there is everything to be said for making the most of American influence and bargaining power to assure that American action toward freer trade is widely matched by corresponding action abroad.

In this connection, however, there is a serious difficulty. A really bold program of multilateral tariff reduction is likely to founder in midstream if the entirely proper emphasis on reciprocity is accompanied by a similar insistence on equal treatment. Where tariff reduction is carried on at a leisurely pace, as it was under the Reciprocal Trade Agreements program, the conflict between reciprocity and equal treatment may not be particularly obvious. By careful bargaining between "principal suppliers" on a commodity-by-commodity basis, the concessions extended to outsiders under the most-favored-nation clause can be kept to a minimum, and no serious friction is likely to arise, particularly where the tariff cuts themselves are modest. The situation is profoundly different, however, where a major multilateral move toward free trade is contemplated. In these circumstances it may be exceedingly difficult to persuade countries to make sweeping tariff reductions if they are required to extend concessions not only to countries which are prepared effectively to reciprocate but also to those which are not. Such reluctance, however regrettable, is entirely understandable, and must be fully taken into account if major new multilateral advances toward free trade are to be achieved.

It is here that there may be an important lesson to be learned from the Six and the Seven. Members of the European Economic Community and the European Free Trade Association have been removing internal trade barriers on a basis of strict reciprocity, the reciprocity taking the form of successive across-the-board tariff cuts under rules which apply uniformly to the members within each group. Two matters are particularly worthy of note. First, the criteria for reciprocity are simple and completely unambiguous. Reciprocity in this context means simply that tariffs are jointly reduced by a given percentage—usually ten per cent—on given dates. Second, the step-by-step concessions are extended only to countries which are jointly engaged in the same program. While this type of behavior is generally regarded as a deviation (though an authorized deviation) from most-favored-nation treatment, it can be looked at, alternatively, as a form of conditional most-favored-nation treatment—the condition of course being that such treatment (ultimately free trade) is extended only to those who reciprocate.

As has often been pointed out, the Trade Expansion Act has

taken one leaf from the Rome Treaty (and from the Stockholm Convention) in the form of provision for across-the-board tariff cuts on a reciprocal basis. It has not, however, taken the other leaf of limiting tariff concessions to countries which are prepared fully to reciprocate in a multilateral program. The Act specifically provides that concessions negotiated with other countries are to be generalized on a most-favored-nation basis—a requirement which in any case is imposed on the United States and other contracting parties by the General Agreement on Tariffs and Trade.

The question now to be considered is whether, in the interest of a vigorous multilateral program of tariff reduction, there is a strong case for modifying the traditional American policy of equal treatment. It will be argued that, subject to certain important qualifications, there is such a case. The first qualification is that there is no case whatever for dispensing completely with the most-favored-nation clause or for adopting a conditional form of the clause in which the conditions—for example, "reciprocity"—are vaguely defined. Either course would be a recipe for chaos, an invitation to endless retaliation, and a long step backward in international commercial relations.

Alternatives to Equal Treatment

But these are not the only possibilities. As the Six and the Seven have shown, it is possible to establish completely unambiguous standards of multilateral reciprocity which effectively rule out what could otherwise be a source of endless bickering and back-tracking. For example, the General Agreement on Tariffs and Trade might be modified in such a way as to permit a group of countries to establish, perhaps in a series of steps, a common tariff ceiling—say ten per cent *ad valorem*—which would apply only to countries prepared to accept this ceiling.[2] Thus, if the group were to include the United States and Canada, American imports from Canada would be subject to duties which could not exceed 10 per cent, while American imports from nonparticipating countries would not be bound by this restriction. In effect, members of the group would have a two-tariff system: a preferential tariff, bound by an agreed ceiling, which would apply to participants; and a nonpreferential tariff, not bound by the ceiling, which would apply to nonparticipants. Such an arrangement would involve not an abandonment, but a modification, of the most-favored-nation clause. Most-favored-nation treatment would be extended, that is to say, to the possibly large number of countries prepared to accept the tariff ceiling.[3]

Of various intermediate possibilities, this one appeals to the author, both because it is highly flexible and because, unlike most other departures from equal treatment, it is not a prescription for utter confusion. But there is another approach which, in the author's view, would be still better if the necessary agreement could be obtained. It is an approach, moreover, which would involve no change in the General Agreement on Tariffs and Trade. If the United States were to join other interested countries in a program to form a customs union or free-trade area, no GATT regulations would be violated, provided the free-trade

[2] Instead of a tariff ceiling, the criterion might be a tariff average. A tariff average, however, would be a much less satisfactory standard for two reasons. In the first place, as shown in Chapter 5, even a very low tariff average—for example, 5 per cent—is consistent with a high degree of protection for particular industries. In the second place, an average which inevitably is derived from hundreds of individual duties provides much more scope than a ceiling for evasion and dispute.

[3] Alternatively and preferably, most-favored-nation treatment could be extended not only to participants, which presumably would be high-income countries, but also to the low-income countries, which could be excused, on infant-industry grounds, from observing the tariff ceiling.

arrangement conformed to GATT standards—i.e., provided internal tariffs were completely removed on "substantially all" internal trade within a "reasonable" length of time.

From an American standpoint, as has been pointed out, the primary objection to participation in regional free-trade arrangements is their exclusiveness. A strictly Atlantic arrangement, for example, would undoubtedly be regarded by the low-income countries as a rich man's club. It is possible, however, to conceive of regional arrangements so broad in their geographic coverage that this essentially political objection would virtually disappear.

This is a possibility which, in the author's opinion, should not be lightly brushed aside. Indeed, it deserves the most careful consideration. If, for example, the "Kennedy round" of tariff negotiations should reveal that the European Economic Community, because of its present domination by President de Gaulle, is willing to make little more than token reductions in its external trade barriers, a creative response by the non-EEC countries might be the creation of a much larger regional arrangement of an "outward-looking" character. It might include as full members the United States, the present EFTA countries, Canada, Australia, New Zealand, and Japan and, as associate members, the countries of Latin America, non-Communist Asia, and non-EEC Africa. As in the European Economic Community, associate members (after a transition period) could be granted free access to the markets of full members, while being permitted, with appropriate safeguards, to retain protection for infant industries. Alternatively, in the interest of solidarity, all participating countries could be given the rank of "full" members, with certain privileges granted to countries where the per capita income was below an agreed level. Such privileges might include access to financial assistance as well as the right to protect infant industries.

The purpose of such an arrangement would be to achieve as

large a free-trade region as possible—including at an early stage, hopefully, the European Economic Community. Although the Community might not be prepared to participate, at least in the beginning, a central objective would be the inclusion of the Community, by one means or another, in the broader grouping. In the meantime the high-income members of the proposed arrangement, after a transition period, would retain tariffs only against nonmembers which, for the time being, would include the Common Market countries. But the sole surpose of imposing tariffs against the Community would be to retain a measure of bargaining power in the hope of negotiating an early marriage between the two groups.

An American Opportunity

Actually, the two approaches just described differ only in degree and, in their intermediate stages, would be virtually indistinguishable. Of the two, the second is clearly the more ambitious in calling for a broad multilateral move toward mutual free trade.

Anything approaching free trade of course goes well beyond the aims of the Trade Expansion Act and, at first glance, would seem an impossible counsel of perfection. Yet it should be remembered that one great country actually pursued such a policy for several decades, and abandoned it only under conditions of *force majeure*. Like certain other legacies of the nineteenth century, free trade in Britain was a victim of the Great Depression, which provided the stern lesson that the economic gains from freedom of trade are little appreciated under conditions of mass unemployment.

But in this sphere we have learned much. The causes of large-scale unemployment—so deep a mystery three decades ago—are now widely understood, and our former inability to deal with this

177

evil can no longer be used as a weighty argument for protection. If we take full advantage of our present economic knowledge, substantially free trade is surely the right goal for American policy, both in the interest of American economic strength and in the interest of free world solidarity. Such a goal should not be pursued frenetically, but approached gradually—and, to the maximum extent, reciprocally—with firm confidence that this is the creative trade policy for as long as anyone can foresee.

Index

179

Council Publications

FOREIGN AFFAIRS (quartery), edited by Hamilton Fish Armstrong.

THE UNITED STATES IN WORLD AFFAIRS (annual). Volumes for 1931, 1932 and 1933, by Walter Lippmann and William O. Scroggs; for 1934-1935, 1936, 1937, 1938, 1939, and 1940, by Whitney H. Shepardson and William O. Scroggs; for 1945–1947, 1947–1948 and 1948–1949, by John C. Campbell; for 1949, 1950, 1951, 1952, 1953 and 1954, by Richard P. Stebbins; for 1955, by Hollis W. Barber; for 1956, 1957, 1958, 1959, 1960, 1961, 1962 and 1963, by Richard P. Stebbins.

DOCUMENTS ON AMERICAN FOREIGN RELATIONS (annual). Volume for 1952 edited by Clarence W. Baier and Richard P. Stebbins; for 1953, and 1954, edited by Peter V. Curl; for 1955, 1956, 1957, 1958 and 1959, edited by Paul E. Zinner; for 1960, 1961, 1962 and 1963, edited by Richard P. Stebbins.

POLITICAL HANDBOOK AND ATLAS OF THE WORLD (annual), edited by Walter H. Mallory.

JAPAN AND THE UNITED STATES IN WORLD TRADE, by Warren S. Hunsberger.

AMERICAN AGENCIES INTERESTED IN INTERNATIONAL AFFAIRS (Fifth Edition), compiled by Donald Wasson.

FOREIGN AFFAIRS BIBLIOGRAPHY 1952–1962, by Henry L. Roberts.

THE DOLLAR IN WORLD AFFAIRS, An Essay in International Financial Policy, by Henry G. Aubrey.

ON DEALING WITH THE COMMUNIST WORLD by George F. Kennan.

FOREIGN AID AND FOREIGN POLICY, by Edward S. Mason.

THE SCIENTIFIC REVOLUTION AND WORLD POLITICS, by Caryl P. Haskins.

AFRICA: A Foreign Affairs Reader, edited by Philip W. Quigg.

THE PHILIPPINES AND THE UNITED STATES: Problems of Partnership, by George E. Taylor.

SOUTHEAST ASIA IN UNITED STATES POLICY, by Russell H. Fifield.

UNESCO: ASSESSMENT AND PROMISE, by George N. Shuster.

THE PEACEFUL ATOM IN FOREIGN POLICY, by Arnold Kramish.

THE ARABS AND THE WORLD: Nasser's Arab Nationalist Policy, by Charles D. Cremeans.

TOWARD AN ATLANTIC COMMUNITY, by Christian A. Herter.

THE SOVIET UNION, 1922–1962: A Foreign Affairs Reader, edited by Philip E. Mosely.

THE POLITICS OF FOREIGN AID: American Experience in Southeast Asia, by John D. Montgomery.

SPEARHEADS OF DEMOCRACY: Labor in the Developing Countries, by George C. Lodge.

LATIN AMERICA: Diplomacy and Reality, by Adolf A. Berle.

THE ORGANIZATION OF AMERICAN STATES AND THE HEMISPHERE CRISIS, by John C. Dreier.

THE UNITED NATIONS: Structure for Peace, by Ernest A. Gross.

THE LONG POLAR WATCH: Canada and the Defense of North America, by Melvin Conant.

ARMS AND POLITICS IN LATIN AMERICA (Revised Edition), by Edwin Lieuwen.

THE FUTURE OF UNDERDEVELOPED COUNTRIES: Political Implications of Economic Development (Revised Edition), by Eugene Staley.

SPAIN AND DEFENSE OF THE WEST: Ally and Liability, by Arthur P. Whitaker.

SOCIAL CHANGE IN LATIN AMERICA TODAY: Its Implications for United States Policy, by Richard N. Adams, John P. Gillin, Allan R. Holmberg, Oscar Lewis, Richard W. Patch, and Charles W. Wagley.

FOREIGN POLICY: THE NEXT PHASE: The 1960s (Revised Edition), by Thomas K. Finletter.

DEFENSE OF THE MIDDLE EAST: Problems of American Policy (Revised Edition), by John C. Campbell.

COMMUNIST CHINA AND ASIA: Challenge to American Policy, by A. Doak Barnett.

FRANCE, TROUBLED ALLY: De Gaulle's Heritage and Prospects, by Edgar S. Furniss, Jr.

THE SCHUMAN PLAN: A Study in Economic Cooperation, 1950–1959, by William Diebold, Jr.

SOVIET ECONOMIC AID: The New Aid and Trade Policy in Underdeveloped Countries, by Joseph S. Berliner.

RAW MATERIALS: A Study of American Policy, by Percy W. Bidwell.

NATO AND THE FUTURE OF EUROPE, by Ben T. Moore.

AFRICAN ECONOMIC DEVELOPMENT, by William Hance.

INDIA AND AMERICA: A Study of Their Relations, by Phillips Talbot and S. L. Poplai.

JAPAN BETWEEN EAST AND WEST, by Hugh Borton, Jerome B. Cohen, William J. Jorden, Donald Keene, Paul F. Langer and C. Martin Wilbur.

NUCLEAR WEAPONS AND FOREIGN POLICY, by Henry A. Kissinger.

MOSCOW-PEKING AXIS: Strength and Strains, by Howard L. Boorman, Alexander Eckstein, Philip E. Mosely and Benjamin Schwartz.

RUSSIA AND AMERICA: Dangers and Prospects, by Henry L. Roberts.

FOREIGN AFFAIRS BIBLIOGRAPHY, 1942–1952, by Henry L. Roberts.